SECRETS OF THE CARPET CLEANING
SUPER-GIANTS

IMPORTANT NOTICE!... REALLY!

Get FREE Stuff!

I have a gift for you to start off our relationship right...

This book talks about a powerful presentation you can use to build value and help you sell your services. You can get your <u>own</u> copy of this presentation **RIGHT NOW** at:

www.offthevan.com/book

Enjoy!

Mark

"SECRETS OF THE CARPET CLEANING SUPER-GIANTS"

THE LEVELS OF SUCCESS PROGRAM

Mark Kennedy's Proven System:
Created For, And Used By... The Largest
And Most Successful Carpet Cleaners On
The Planet!

Mark Kennedy

Table Of Contents

Disclaimer

This book, this program, the author, and any affiliates, do not offer any financial advice. Nor do they recommend that the information contained in this program or manual be construed in any such way. Mark Kennedy, Millennium Business Strategies Inc. and any and all affiliates insist that any financial action taken by, (on or behalf of) the purchaser or reader of this material, is at the INDIVIDUALS OWN RISK and PROFESSIONAL FINANCIAL ADVICE should always be sought after, relating to matters of this nature.

This manual and system is not designed or intended to give you legal advice. If you have any questions regarding the legality or consequences of any strategy contained in this system, you are advised to seek guidance from a qualified advisor of your own choosing. Mark Kennedy, Millennium Business Strategies Inc., and their associates or affiliates are not responsible in any way, for any consequence, direct or indirect, from using any strategy or system contained herein. Results are not guaranteed and may vary. All examples are for illustration only and any resemblance to any person, living or dead is purely coincidental and unintentional. You agree to assume all responsibility for using any strategy or approach recommended by Mark Kennedy in person, in this book, or in this system.

Acknowledgements

Thanking everyone that I should, is absolutely impossible. Many people, not just the ones I mention here, have had a part in shaping my life, my career, and in bringing this book to you. These words don't begin to express my appreciation to those people that have made a difference in my life. Thank you to all of you.

To Felicia… Thank you: Most of all, you deserve my thanks for your unwavering support and belief.

To my sons… Thank you: Christopher and Caleb, your spirit and goodness make it all worthwhile.

To my friends… Thank you: To Robert Williamson, a true 'partner-in-crime', for many discussions about any topic imaginable. To Jeff Koonce for being my sounding board, my conscience, and my dear friend. To Dan and Paula Dahlin, dear friends with whom I've had many interesting late-night conversations. To John Mosher with whom I've been honored to walk down many roads.

To my clients… Thank you: Working with all of you over the last ten years has been an honor and a privilege. I have learned from you all, and I hope that the seeds of your success can help to inspire others, through the pages of this book.

Special Thanks… Thank you: To Michael and Anne Jatoft, for being a great example of a successful husband and wife team, and good friends to boot. To Bob Spalten for his support and friendship and many, memorable moments. To Jay Kennedy, one of the best examples I've ever known of a man who has true heart…who knows who he is and who knows how to take care of his family, I truly respect you my friend. To Larry and Tryna Cooper for having the courage to bring fire-walking to the Connections Conference.

To my teachers… Thank you: To Tolly Burkan for teaching me how to write in the middle of the night, and how to apply spirituality to everyday life. To Margaret Croce for helping me to find my voice.

To my past partners… Thank you: To Danny Duran, what an adventure, what a ride! To Clark Lovrein, the 'Mark and Clark show' is still a great memory, I learned a lot with you.

To the management team and employees of my cleaning company… Thank you: We made a difference and had a great fifteen-year ride.

1.
Why You Absolutely MUST Read This Book In Order To Avoid Ruining Your Business And Your Financial Life

I have a question for you: If you were in a trap, (a business trap) that would ruin your business and your financial life, but there was a simple, proven, step-by-step way out, would you want to know about it?

Would you?

What if you really didn't believe you were trapped at all?

I only ask because Chances are, **<u>YOU'RE TRAPPED!</u>**

I mean right now.

The very nature of traps is that people that are walking into them don't realize it until it's too late.

I don't want this to happen to you, and let's face it... neither do you!

This book explains exactly what this trap is… why over 90% of carpet cleaners fall into it… and most importantly, exactly what you can do to keep yourself, your business, and your family, safe.

Now that opening may be a little dramatic, I'll grant you that, but the 'trap' I'm talking about is very real, and it's all around you.

In fact, it happens to most carpet cleaners, and they don't even realize it's happening until it's too late!

The next time you're at a carpet cleaning convention, or a training class, look around.

Over 90% of the people there… hardworking people who care about their employees, their customers, and their businesses, will fall victim to a <u>fatal flaw</u>, a weakness in their business that will prevent them from ever being free.

But that's not the real problem.

The real problem is, YOU could be one of them…

And not even know it!

People with families, with hopes and dreams… trapped! Living a life of struggle and suffering, never able to get their heads above water. Forced to run and run, and it's never enough.

You can end up caught… trapped in a situation where you have no options and no control, and can't get your business to give you any real quality of life.

Thankfully, that doesn't have to happen to you. <u>Even if it already is happening right now</u>! You don't have to end up that way.

This book is about success as a carpet cleaner, and how to achieve the KIND of success you're probably looking for.

It's about several powerful ways to achieve a quality of life and a quality within your business that you can truly be proud of. It's about how your carpet cleaning business can set you free.

It's about how you can become one of the few truly successful carpet cleaners. It's about really getting your dreams. That may sound hokey, but it's true.

It's not automatic though. It won't happen by accident. You can't wait for this to just fall in your lap, because it won't.

It's also not impossibly hard... you just have to know what to do and you can easily set yourself up to be free and wealthy.

This all comes from a change in the way you look at things. This is a difference in perspective in the way you see your business, and what it's supposed to do for you. It is a vision, a way of looking at your business that you probably don't have right now.

My purpose in writing this book is to show you that vision, that path... a way out of the trap.

A business is really a vehicle.

What I mean by that is that it's supposed to take you somewhere. It's supposed to do something for you.

Imagine for a moment that you could take a journey back in time, to when you first started your business. Do you remember what that was like?

It was a very exciting time, full of possibility. Oh, you were definitely nervous, and maybe a little scared, but you were also hopeful.

You anticipated your success. You relished the idea of being free.

You looked forward to being financially independent, of being the master of your own destiny, of having tons of options, each one more exciting and more promising than the one before it.

Maybe you weren't trying to be wealthy, but I'll bet you WERE trying to be free.

Spending time with your kids. Taking the vacations that other people just can't take. Really building something real for yourself, after all, this is your life, and you only get one shot at this. It only makes sense to really make it count, doesn't it?

That's what your business was supposed to do for you. That's what you wanted. That's what you sacrificed and worked for.

Fast-forward to right now.

Unfortunately, if you talk to most carpet cleaners, their lives have become a never-ending series of struggles... one after another, after another, after another.

Maybe you can relate.

Even if things aren't really all that bad, they're not all that good either.

These people aren't free. In fact they're anything but free!

> Most carpet cleaners are still trying to hang on to that vision of freedom, but it's always a vision that will happen sometime in the future… at some vague time when 'things get better', it's almost never right now.

Even if you're relatively successful, that success usually comes from paying a heavy price of almost ridiculous amounts of work.

And there are other problems. Finding good help, keeping quality high, getting a steady flow of business, paying taxes, insurance, bills, the list goes on and on.

The business basically chases you around the room.

It feels like being completely out of control… like running in front of a giant snowball, that's thundering down a mountainside. You can't stop, because if you do, you're doomed!

All you can do is keep running and running, faster and faster. All thoughts of freedom and independence have long since been completely abandoned.

Your business can become all-consuming. Taking time away from your kids, your family… all the things that you once thought were so important.

In fact, it takes time away from the very things that were the reason you started your business in the first place!

If you're successful, making good money, you still may not be free of this trap. In fact, surprisingly you just might be in deeper than anyone else!

You'll see in a little while that I'm uniquely qualified to show you the path to success in this industry.

And I'm going to show you a way to quickly and easily retire rich, in a much shorter time than you probably think.

But right now, let's talk about this trap...

What is it, and how does it happen?

"The Three Big Traps That Imprison Over 90% Of Carpet Cleaners:"

There are three parts to this trap. Any one of them can stop you cold. Unfortunately, many carpet cleaners are struggling with all three.

The three parts to this trap are:

1. **You are unable to sell the business because of the way it's structured.**
2. **You are unable to grow because there is not enough money to hire or grow.**
3. **Low profit**

Let's take a look at these three and learn how they happen and why and how they'll stop you.

Carpet Cleaner Trap #1 - Unable to sell the business because of the way it's structured

Let's start by agreeing on something: Let's assume that you have a great little business. (1 to 3 vans) You've got plenty of happy customers and you stay very, very busy.

You make good money and you charge fair prices.

You really care about your customers because you run into them in the grocery store. You never want to be in a position where you have to hide, or hang your head because of the way you've treated somebody.

So you guarantee your work, and you educate yourself. You go to classes and you never stop learning.

You may even buy a business success package or two from your friendly carpet cleaning guru. These are usually about 'marketing' and usually the gurus who sell them promise you great results.

Based on this description, many would think you are the very model of a successful carpet cleaner.

Life is great!

So what's the catch? Where's the trap I keep talking about?

Here's the thing to realize: At some point, someday, somehow, for some reason... you're going to need to sell your business.

- It might just be because you're tired...

- I hope it's not because of a medical condition.
- Maybe it's time to retire.
- Maybe you're just bored to death and you decide you want to do something else for a change. (Burnout!)
- I really, really hope it's not because someone in your family needs the money to deal with some catastrophe.

My point is, it's not IF you ever decide to sell your business... it's WHEN! It might be years down the road because of something you've planned, or it could be next month because of something unexpected.

It could be because of something awful that happened to you or it could be because of something great. But someday, for SOME reason, you're going to want to sell.

Heck, maybe you sell it to your kids for a dollar.

The one thing I know for sure is that your business, the one you worked so hard to build, is going to be sold some day, for SOME reason!

And the real question is, what is your business worth?

Maybe you're not thinking of selling your business once... in fact, maybe you want to franchise it and sell it again and again, to many different people.

Or maybe you want to set it up so you can keep it and make money from it.

It doesn't really matter what your plans are, the point is that it really needs to be set up so that it can be sold or you can't be free of it... and again, what's it worth?

Now before we go any further down this road, I know what you may be thinking.

You're thinking that sure, you actually MAY sell your business SOMEDAY, but that day isn't going to be here for a long, long, time, so why worry about it now?

So what's the problem here? Why do I seem so convinced that you might have a problem selling it?

The problem comes from the way you almost certainly set it up in the first place.

Let's assume you're like most small carpet cleaners. That means that you probably have many loyal clients, which seems like it would be great. In fact, it probably took you years to build that up.

If you bought a marketing package and followed it, that probably made the problem WORSE!

The problem actually is that your clients ARE so loyal... They're loyal to YOU, not to some new owner that you just sold your business to.

Your clients like you and trust you and I'm sure you have a great relationship with most of them. But as soon as you bring someone new into your business as an owner, all bets are off!

That relationship that you spent years building is over, and YOU ended it!

They don't know this new owner at all, and chances are you're going to be a hard act to follow.

In most cases, the 'value' that a new owner buys, simply doesn't exist, because what the new owner is trying to buy is that relationship. And relationships can't be sold.

You're almost a victim of your own success. Precisely because you were so good, it makes it almost impossible for someone else to come in and take things over and do any kind of a good job of giving your customers what they came to expect from you.

Unfortunately, what that really means is that if you sell your business, the only thing you really have to sell is a bunch of worn-out, used-up junk (equipment).

The customers won't be loyal to the new owner, so there really isn't nearly as much value there as most people think.

Think about it from the new owners' perspective: If you have to build a relationship with a bunch of customers, why not start out on your own? Why pay top-dollar to buy a business from someone else if you can't buy the relationship with the customers?

As if that weren't bad enough, many times the new owner, in all their wisdom, decides that you couldn't possibly have known anything about what you were doing when you were running the business, so they decide to change everything!

A successful business is a balancing act. Change a few critical things, and the whole thing falls down, and it can happen really fast.

www.levelsofsuccessprogram.com

Another fact is that most small service businesses are sold on contract, where the owner carries terms and basically finances the purchase for a time period.

The failure rate for this type of sale is really high… in many cases, the new owner runs the business into the ground and then says he can't make the payments. By the time you get your business back, it's been gutted and ruined.

Game over.

But What If You Don't Have Any Intention Of Selling?

The very things that make your business sellable are the things that will probably not make you ever want to sell it!

If your business runs without a lot of constant supervision and headache from you, you'd almost be crazy to ever sell it, but almost no one sets their business up this way.

If the relationship exists between the customers and your business, instead of between the customers and YOU… If your business has strong systems in place that guarantee the customer has an incredible experience and if anything goes wrong, everything is taken care of quickly and to the customer's complete satisfaction…You COULD sell it… but why would you?

I have trained hundreds of carpet cleaners, and very few companies ever get to this place, but those that do have it all. They have freedom, options, profit, money, and time to enjoy it all.

(That's really what this book is about, how to set your business up that way so you can get those results.)

There has been a lot of talk about the value of systemizing your business... the problem is, nobody really tells you how to do it.

Once a business has really been set up in a way that it is massively profitable, and there is a structure in place that allows you to easily manage everything that goes on within the business, it becomes a cash cow! It pays you just because you own it.

What I'm saying is, you don't have to be there to earn that money... and that's what I really want to show you how to do.

I want to show you how to set up your company so you have the money coming in on a regular basis, you have the ability to give it to your kids, to sell it to someone else, to keep it... absolutely whatever you want to do.

At that point, you have options. (And interestingly enough, your business will actually be worth a whole lot more BECAUSE it is now sellable.)

You didn't start this to be a carpet cleaner, you did it because you wanted to own a business that would allow you to succeed. For whatever reason, you chose carpet cleaning as your vehicle, and that's fine, it can serve you well.

Of course if you sell this type of business, you'll be able to sell it for top-dollar because all of a sudden you don't really have to sell it to another carpet cleaner. You can sell it to an investor, because your business now meets all the criteria for a real investment. (Someone can put money into it and get money back out of it, without working 90 hours a week!)

If most carpet cleaners had to sell their businesses, they'd really be selling a job, because for their businesses to run, it takes constant, never-ending focus from the owner.

Let me be clear about something here: When I talk about being able to leave the business, I'm not talking about being able to take two-weeks off, I'm talking about being able to spend massive amounts of time (months) away from the business and still have it pay you for being the owner.

Without this type of structure, you don't ever end up making any real money, and if you do, you have to work your tail off to do it. (You trade your life for it) If you're ever sick, or hurt, or you decide to take some time off, you're basically unemployed.

Carpet Cleaner Trap #2 - Unable to grow because there is not enough money to hire or grow

Many carpet cleaners talk about how they'll grow their company and hire someone to help out. Unfortunately there are problems here that most carpet cleaners don't realize.

When you started out, you probably built your business one customer at a time. This happened at a time when overhead was very low.

You probably had a van and a cell phone, and that was about it. You worked out of your garage, and your office was a spare bedroom or the kitchen table.

What I'm getting at is that you didn't have a receptionist, at least not one you were paying anyway. (Your wife may have answered the phone) You had no outside office, no utilities, no real marketing campaigns, often no insurance, or work comp, or payroll... basically your overhead was pretty much nothing!

If you're operating like this, and you do a job for $200, you really do get to keep most of that money.

But here's what happens: You may decide to grow your company and hire someone else to help out. If that technician just takes over your work, you'll have to pay him, and there usually isn't enough left over for you to live on, so you have to grow.

What you really need is twice the amount of work, since you now have twice the people, but that's not how work comes in. To really sustain it, you need twice the number of customers, and you just can't buy those overnight.

Besides that, if you go through a slow time, and every business does, the payroll can be a killer!

Not only do you have to start giving a lot of the money you're earning to your employee, but very quickly your other expenses rise as well.

It's not long before you need more cell phones, another van, all the equipment that goes on that van, and very quickly you'll need a place to work that's not your kitchen table or your living room.

Your expenses shoot through the roof!

Meanwhile, your business is growing slowly... one customer at a time!

What this means is that you are working more than twice as hard, and you're probably making less money.

Think about this: The average carpet cleaning company, and I'm talking about one of the larger companies here, makes somewhere between 10% and 20% profit, with 15% being about the average.

Two things: First of all, most of these guys know what they're doing.

Second, they do have a lot of expenses that you probably don't, but they also have some economy of scale that you don't have. They can buy things cheaper, and negotiate harder with their suppliers and vendors because they buy in bulk.

So let's say you're making $50,000 a year right now as an owner/operator, and you decide to hire some people and grow.

As an owner/operator, let's say you're bringing in about $70,000 total revenue, in order to keep that $50,000 profit. (The other $20,000 is going to pay for your van, your cleaning supplies, and your cell phone bill)

When you hire people to do the work, and get an office, your profit margin, (in other words what you get to keep) can easily drop to 20% (and I'm being generous here, it could be a lot lower than that).

For you to make that same $50,000 under the new system, you'd have to be bringing in $250,000 instead of $70,000! (20% of $250,000 = $50,000)

If you aren't particularly good at controlling and managing money, and your profit margin is 10%, you'll need to bring in $500,000 to make that same $50,000 you were before. (10% of $500,000 = $50,000)

In other words, you get to grow three to seven times the size you are right now (at least!) and you don't get to make an extra dime!

Pretty exciting, huh?

Now, if you're still cleaning and working as a technician on one of the vans, you'd get to add what you'd pay a technician on top of your profit, but if you're busting out carpet cleaning jobs all day long, how are you going to grow the business?

With all the investments in marketing, advertising for help, training, etc., what will happen is you're personally going to take a pay cut, and probably for a long time, in order to grow your business.

Finally, after a ton of work and grinding out long days doing everything, you'll get to a point where you are even with where you were before you started, and after even more time, you might actually get ahead.

But can you afford to take a substantial pay cut for a couple of years?

Most carpet cleaners can't afford to do this and so they stay small, and as a result they can't build anything that will ever get them free… in other words, they are trapped.

They are small and their income is limited and they have to physically work to make money.

Many carpet cleaners don't realize this at all until it's too late, and when they try to grow, they end up going broke.

The extra expenses quickly eat up anything that might be left over, and before they know it, they are in a hole too deep to get out of.

Carpet Cleaner Trap #3 - Low profit

Most carpet cleaners struggle… they don't flourish. Just talk to other carpet cleaners and you'll find that very few of them are really financially comfortable.

Most of them are in trouble. Even if they are getting by, they are one slow season away from financial ruin.

Things go in cycles. You'll see a few years of relative abundance, followed by a recession. You'll see interest rates go up, and then they come back down again.

What happens to businesses when things slow down, is that the weakest businesses, go out of business. The strong survive. This isn't a bad thing unless you happen to be running one of the weak businesses!

The simple truth is that if you are making more profit from each job, you are immensely stronger than a competitor who is making less profit.

Profit is how you win the game in business. Profit is what a business is designed to do. It is the scorecard.

The first two items that 'trap' you are very real, and they absolutely will stop you if you let them.

Profit, however, is how you buy your way out of the trap.

* Low profit will ruin your life because you aren't making enough money to survive on.

- It will also keep you in this awful place because you won't be able to buy your way out of the trap!

If you're making enough profit, you can afford to build the kind of business you know you should.

All too often, carpet cleaners have some idea of what they probably should be doing, but they can't seem to actually build the businesses they want because they aren't able to afford to do what they want to do.

Sometimes what they want, and what they actually get... are miles apart!

These owners often can't figure out what they're doing wrong. They are running as hard and as fast as they can, trying desperately to make money, but there is just no way they can keep up.

Maybe you can relate.

You have to have some common sense about all of this, of course. You can't take every extra dime you earn and buy toys with it, and then wonder why there isn't enough money left over to build your business... you do need to invest in your business.

One of the worst things is when someone starts to get in trouble with their business, and they end up in a hole.

Now, not only do they need to be profitable and keep up with everything... they need to dig out of the hole they're in as well! This is tough.

Again, not making enough money is the primary cause of becoming stuck, because it makes you weak and vulnerable.

This is the justification for taking jobs that you know you shouldn't take.

The desperate need of more money is the reason you'll do things you know you shouldn't... maybe compromise your values. Maybe cut corners on jobs in order to make them profitable... and justify it all because you need to make more money.

This is why you'll miss the important things in life, the school games, the plays, the concerts, the vacations, because in order to get by you have to work almost constantly... and if you don't, you feel guilty.

It's easy to get so busy struggling for a dollar, that you end up losing out on many important things in life... Irreplaceable things.

But above all else, you'll be trapped. Stuck in a very uncomfortable place. Always looking to the future for a time when things will get better, but that time never seems to come.

Poverty and desperation never lead to the very best in people.

Most of this book is about getting out of these traps and keeping yourself from falling into them in the first place. But before you can learn about the way out, there is one thing you have to do right now.

You can't keep lying to yourself.

It may dull the pain a little bit to hang on to hope. It may make you feel better... but the future won't be any different than the past unless you change some things. You've got to be willing to own your own results, and if there is a problem, you've got to admit that you have it.

Sticking your head in the sand won't help you get anywhere, and yet it's perfectly natural. No one wants to admit they have a problem. Our pride is involved.

Let me clarify this: One of the biggest problems in our industry is the phenomenon known as 'burnout'. This is where you just can't bring yourself to care anymore. The business suffers, you suffer, your family suffers... Burnout is really a form of depression. It is caused by the loss of hope.

When I talk about not lying to yourself, I'm not saying to give up hope. But you also can't fool yourself about where you really are and expect things to change if you don't do something different to change them.

Does This Apply To You?

Some people have done quite well for themselves in this industry. They aren't living a life of desperation. In fact they're doing quite well. They've gotten themselves to a point where things are pretty comfortable. What about these people... what if this is you?

First of all, congratulations! You've done well.

I don't want to take anything away from you, but you could still be trapped.

All three of the 'traps' could still apply to you even if you're doing well right now.

When someone says they're 'doing well', what they usually mean is that they are making money. Hopefully they also include some quality of life in their measurement of how they are doing as well.

Let's remember the three traps:

1. **Unable to sell the business because of the way it's structured.**
2. **Unable to grow because there is not enough money to hire or grow.**
3. **Low profit**

These can still apply to you, and here's why:

- First of all, you might not be aware of how difficult it will be to get what you think your business is worth out of your business because you haven't tried to sell it yet.
- You may not have gone through all the growing pains because you may not have really tried to grow.
- You might be making enough money right now.

So here's the deal. Most often when someone claims these don't apply to them, they have a smaller company, they don't want to sell, they don't want to grow, and they are making plenty of money...

So what's the problem? Why can't they just stay right where they are and be happy?

First of all, because it won't last... it can't! At some point you're going to have to sell. There is a reason that there aren't that many 50-plus year old carpet cleaners out there, and someday you WILL find out why. You're going to have to come off of that van someday.

But that is then and this is now... why worry about it now?

Because you are stuck, that's why. What you've almost certainly got is a good-paying job, working for yourself.

Let's be clear, you don't have a business.

A business can be looked at as an investment. An owner can put money into it and it can make money for them.

A true business requires investment, because it IS an investment. But it is an investment of money, not life... not time.

If you buy stock in Microsoft, you will pay money for it, and hopefully you'll make money back from it. But you don't have to show up for work at Microsoft on Monday morning to make your money!

Microsoft is a business. There are people that show up for work on Monday, but they are the employees, not the stockholders... not the owner. The owner has money invested in it, that's all.

If you have a true money-making business, people will line up to buy it or to invest in it because it isn't a job. It's a true investment, and people are always looking for good investments.

This means it will be easier to sell and you'll be able to sell it for more money. That's pretty specific don't you think?

This affects you because you also probably don't have the ability to step away from your company, at least most people don't, so they aren't really free.

But what's so bad about that. Maybe you're quite happy doing what you are doing.

Two things:

First, just because your business is set up to sell, doesn't mean you have to sell it. What it DOES mean is that your business is worth more BECAUSE it is set up to sell, and as a result you are in a better place... you have more options.

Second, your whole work-world isn't set up so that it falls apart if you don't show up for work everyday. Building an organization that runs without you is the most liberating thing you could ever do.

Then, if someday something happens and you aren't able to show up for work the way you did when you were 23, it's still okay. You still have your little cash machine chugging away at full steam.

There is one more thing— The third trap of low profit. No matter how much you are making right now, you could almost certainly be making much more money than you are right now from your business.

Now maybe that isn't that important to you, but you could use the extra money to buy the very best equipment, donate to a cause you think is worthy, pay your employees more... I don't have to make the list for you, there is a lot that you could do with 'extra' money.

A lot of people are hung up on that. They feel that making money is wrong somehow. If this describes you, get over it, make the money anyway, and donate it to something you think is worthwhile. But put some of it back into your business because then it can grow stronger.

Every now and then I'll run into someone who is 'the most successful carpet cleaner they know'. This person is doing better than many other carpet cleaners they know. They are probably making more money than their parents did... probably make more than most of their friends, and are probably a little arrogant about it... cocky.

These people are usually so busy congratulating themselves and patting themselves on the back that they don't bother to notice that they are really in trouble. Next thing you know, they are fighting to stay alive.

This book is about building a strong healthy business. Can you see the danger in claiming that your business is already strong and healthy enough?

It's like the smoker that claims that his smoking isn't that bad and waits until he has a health crisis before he takes any action to get healthy. Maybe he'll be okay and maybe he won't, but it's not the smart thing to do.

All I'm saying is: Be careful, and be aware if you are justifying not needing to do this. What could possibly be wrong in having a stronger, more valuable business? Isn't that the smart thing to do? Doesn't that make sense, to build something strong and valuable for yourself and your family?

The Levels Of Success Concept And How It Can Set You Free

This is where I'm going to challenge you... It's also where I expect to lose a few readers, because this might scare you...

There are four types, or levels, of carpet cleaning companies. No matter how big or how small your business is right now, you are somewhere along this path.

Some people never grow their companies to a large size, and that's fine, you don't have to. The point is, your company lies somewhere along the path from a level one, to a level four company.

This is important to understand so that you can understand exactly what it will take to get your company to a point where it can make you financially free.

Level One	Owner/Operator, basically a guy with a van and a cell phone. Most carpet cleaners have level one companies.
Level Two	An Owner/Operator with 1 to 3 vans. There usually are not many other employees other than technicians. Occasionally someone may be running the office and answering the phone
Level Three	These companies are large enough to have a general manager, several employees, and often bring in a million dollars or more in revenue each year
Level Four	These companies have departmental managers running each department and can bring in 5-million-plus dollars each year. Some of the largest bring in close to 20 million each year and have well over a hundred employees.

So the real question here is: How does this affect you, and why is it important?

> Certain things have to happen for a business to get to a point where the owner is truly free of it. At that point, the business serves the owner... but before that point you could pretty much say the owner serves the business.

The problem of making enough profit (money) is solved using a sales system that you're about to learn about. It works so well, it's almost unbelievable.

But the problems of structure, and of everything revolving around the owner, can't be solved by just making more money. Don't get me wrong, you'll make more money than you ever have, but you won't really solve the problem of having to actually work as a carpet cleaner unless you do some other things.

In order for you to get off the van and become an owner/investor, instead of an owner/operator, your company has to be big enough to afford to hire a general manager.

You also need a strong, well-defined structure in place that will allow you to stay in control even though you're not there every day.

This doesn't happen until you build at least a level three company.

If you go back and look at the chart, you'll find that means that you have at least a 1 million-dollar company— And that is what scares people.

You might have a small company right now and you may have been at it for ten years or more. The simple truth is you may have no idea of how to build a company of that size.

Many people have absolutely no desire to build a company that big. If you ask them why, they'll talk about what an awful pain employees are, and how hard it has been for them with just a few of them. Most of them would rather have painful dental work than have to deal with any more employees!

This is actually a symptom of the trap we talked about earlier. If you try and grow without clear systems that will allow you to hold your employees accountable, what you end up with is a nightmare.

Of course you're going to base your opinions on your own experience, what else would you do?

If the only thing you've known is that employees equal pain, no one would blame you for not wanting any!

There is a path through this however. It's not hard to do, it's just that relatively few people ever find it.

When people start their businesses, they are forced to make a lot of decisions.

- They have to decide how much to charge.
- They have to decide how to promote their business
- They have to decide who their target market is going to be
- They have to decide how to reach their target market
- They have to make all sorts of decisions about the 'model' they are going to use for their business

Unfortunately, all these decisions were made in a vacuum. What I mean by that is that these decisions often weren't made with complete information.

People talk to a few other carpet cleaners and maybe someone at their local distributorship and they make their decisions based on what they are advised by these 'experts'.

Nothing against the distributors, but many of them are failed carpet cleaners... and we've already discussed how most regular carpet cleaners out there are quite literally starving to death!

What kind of advice can these people possibly give you that's any good?

When you started your business, did you travel the country and interview the largest and most successful carpet cleaners in the world and make decisions about your business based on that? Probably not.

It's impossible to build a strong, successful company on a structure and foundation that can't support it.

The path from wherever you are right now to being an absentee owner of a million-dollar-plus carpet cleaning company is easier than you think, and it exists. In fact, that's what this book is about.

It is possible to get there in as little as ten years, even if you're starting from almost nothing right now.

Along the way, you'll have fun, make money, and you'll become one of the industry leaders, breathing the 'rarified air' of the few carpet cleaners that have a business that can truly make them a millionaire!

If you have a million-dollar-plus business that is extremely profitable, you'll be able to sell it anytime you want for a lot of money… IF, and only if, it's structured so that you're really selling a business and not just a job.

If an owner can buy it and not have to spend 90 hours a week running it… it behaves like an investment and it will pay the owner, whoever that is, whether that's you or someone else, for just owning it and spending just a little time each week running it. It becomes a profit machine.

The business can be paying rent for a building which of course YOU own! So basically this business is buying you some high-priced commercial real estate while it's making you money at the same time.

How much money can this business make you? If the business is bringing in 1 million dollars and you're making 15% profit from it, that's $150,000 a year, in addition to the equity in the business, (which you could sell) in addition to the equity in the commercial building (which you could also sell).

The business can also pay for other things like vehicles, insurance, vacations, and many other 'perks'.

This is the only reason to have a business in my opinion.

Why go through all the hassle if you can't have the rewards? Why spend years of your life struggling to make ends meet and then have to sell your business for pennies on the dollar because you failed to set it up right in the first place?

[Of course there is one other path as well. It is possible to take these strategies and use them to charge top-dollar and stay small.

The only way to make this work, is to live very cheaply and invest as much as you can into something that will provide you with financial security. In my experience, most don't have the discipline to do this. In fact, most carpet cleaners don't have the ability to do extra work.

For most, pretty much every dime they earn gets spent as soon as they earn it!

Because of this, this book will focus on building a business. Just remember that you can take these same strategies and use them to make more money as an owner-operator.]

Why Don't More Carpet Cleaners Do This?

Most carpet cleaners don't know how to do this. They can't find the path, often because no one they know has ever done it, or if they do know them, they are the competition.

Even if you could travel to some of the larger carpet cleaning companies in the world and talk to the owners, you might get some insights, but I can almost guarantee you wouldn't get the whole story. Why?

Because you wouldn't get the 'dirt'.

Everyone's got dirt. The challenges that they hope no one else knows about.

I've seen 'successful' owners of large companies give tours of their operation and show the visitor how great everything was... the problem was, the whole time, the owner of the large company was overdrawn and facing lawsuits!

What the visitor really wanted was information about how to handle the inevitable problems of business. What the visitor got was a trip to a fairy-tale world that doesn't really exist!

This incredible dream… this vision of owning a million-dollar company that is well-run and structured, can be done. But honestly few people will really do it.

For most, it just seems too unbelievable, too big to accomplish. And yet people do it everyday.

I'm looking for people to take that journey with me… yes, I'm talking to YOU.

It's not typical. What I mean is, it's not typical for most carpet cleaners to achieve those results. Most will never rise above the stage where they are struggling to stay alive.

This really isn't that surprising when you think about it. Most carpet cleaners don't have any background in business, and even people with those backgrounds usually don't have any experience in structuring systems, compensation strategies, and management models.

But the business we're talking about needs all of those things, the question is, how do you get all of that stuff and how do you understand it all?

I'm going to show you. The truth is, anything you don't know, is hard. Brain surgery is easy… if you know how to do it!

Most carpet cleaners don't really even know what they don't know. The things that they think will fix the problems in their businesses often won't work at all, or they might only be temporary, or might just be a band-aid for a much larger problem that the owner doesn't really realize they have.

Most carpet cleaners take whatever knowledge and background they have... and they do the best they can.

That's all any of us can do. The difference is that a few of them are searching for a better way. They are aware that the solutions they are using right now might not be the best ones.

If you can get your head around the idea that it just might be possible for you to own a company of that size, and that type, a whole new world of possibility opens up for you.

Your competition definitely doesn't want you thinking that way. If they knew, it would scare them to death! But this is possible for you, if you let it be possible.

In the next section, I'm going to answer some questions about who I am, and why I'm qualified to talk to you about all of this, as well as tell you exactly why I'd even want to!

I think it's important that you know what my motivations are— that you know what's in it for me.

We're also going to cover some principles that we'll use to leverage your way out of the traps we talked about earlier. You'll learn some interesting new ways of looking at some familiar problems, and some of them might surprise you.

But first let's recap what we've talked about so far. These are the main points I want you to get before we move on.

If you are the typical carpet cleaner:

- Just getting by is a struggle
- You have no clear step-by-step path you can follow to success
- You have no plan and no clear idea of what success in this business really means
- You made critical decisions about your business at a time when you had very little knowledge, and probably didn't get the right advice from the right people
- You are trapped by low prices
- You are afraid to raise prices too much or too fast
- You use the fact that you have low overhead to justify your low prices so you can claim you are still making money
- If you quit working in your business for any length of time, you basically quit making money
- If you quit working in your business, things fall apart
- Other than maybe being away for a couple of weeks for a quick vacation, you can't afford to be away from your business
- You hate managing employees and have no effective way to really keep them accountable
- You are in business, but you don't have a business background, especially when it comes to business modeling and systems analysis
- Your business needs systems, you know that, but you aren't really sure what a system would look like, you figure it's just a written-down procedure

- You sometimes have trouble clinging to the hope that someday things are going to get better and everything is going to be alright
- You think growing your company consists of getting more work and hiring some more people
- You can't seem to make everything work the way it should, something always seems wrong
- You have cash-flow problems on a regular basis
- You feel stuck
- You don't have nearly enough in retirement
- You sometimes feel you aren't really running the kind of business you wish you could
- You take jobs you know you probably shouldn't because you need the money
- Sometimes you feel like a loser
- You sometimes avoid balancing the checkbook or paying bills because you know you don't have enough money and you don't want to get depressed.
- Sometimes you get depressed because you avoid paying your bills or balancing your checkbook
- You feel out of control
- The stakes are really high, but you're not sure you're winning the game
- You compare yourself to others that you hang around with and you tell yourself that you're really not doing that bad
- When you compare income with others, you use your gross revenue before expenses because it makes you feel better

- The whole business end seems confusing and you're unsure of what you should do
- The 'lack' that you experience in your life is taking a toll on you, your wife or significant other, and your family

If you can relate to several of these, I don't have to tell you, you're trapped!

These problems and the three traps don't usually stand alone, they intertwine and work together to hold a business back from what it could be.

I want you to grab onto a vision for something better.

Most carpet cleaners aren't very good at management... and why would they be, they've probably never done it before?

In fact, why would YOU be good at systems analysis and building a business if you don't have a degree and years of experience doing either one?

All right, let's move on and talk about some principles that we can use to make you a millionaire carpet cleaner.

When It Comes To Your Business, You Are Probably Your Own Worst Enemy

Let's talk about probably the greatest limit to your success you'll ever face:

You.

A business is always a reflection of the owner, and there are no exceptions.

There is a powerful principle that has been proven time and time again by general experience and by psychology departments. It is a general truth, there are exceptions, but they are rare.

> How you do something is how you do everything.

Every business, even the big ones, grow until that growth is stopped by the owner.

Now I don't mean that you decide that you couldn't possibly handle any more success and you decide to stop growing… This is more subtle than that.

It's more like you fail to check on things that you really should be checking on and quality suffers so you lose some customers…

Or, you get too busy to take the time to do enough marketing and as a result business slows down during a normally busy part of the year.

Or you put off making a critical decision and it backfires on you.

This stuff is usually all unconscious, no one ever means to do it, and there are usually very good reasons (excuses) for it. And yet, if the quality doesn't get checked, or the marketing doesn't get done, the business suffers, and it doesn't matter how good the reason was.

Bottom line, running your own business means that you have to assume a truly massive responsibility, because literally everything that must happen usually involves you in some way or other.

This level of responsibility is tough to swallow because it can very easily feel like failure or like you're taking on burdens you shouldn't have to. Most people don't really take responsibility for their lives, and this is no exception.

Most owners start out, have a little success, get busy... and then from that point on, they don't ever manage to really do what they should.

The business suffers, and they never get to where they really wanted to go because their business was never able to take them there. Unfortunately the real reason was that they never gave it the chance!

My point in telling you this is that the success you want is probably beyond an obstacle and that obstacle is usually you... in some form or another.

If you forget what you think you know and look at this with an open mind, you'll find it's true.

This really matters because you can spend massive amounts of time and energy fixing the business and fixing everything around you, trying desperately to change things, but if you don't change you... then nothing else really changes and you don't get the result you were after.

This isn't the only way you can stop yourself however.

There are three things that nearly every one of us carries inside us that can make success in our lives difficult if not impossible.

1. Fear
2. Limiting Beliefs
3. Low Self-Esteem

Fear can stop you cold— and many people are afraid. No one wants to lose what they've worked for, or starve, or be humiliated or embarrassed. Unfortunately fear can prevent us from even trying things that might be unfamiliar.

Every one of us evaluates everything based on our experience. This is only common sense. The problem occurs when we have pre-conceived notions about what is true.

These beliefs then act as filters, filtering out things that might contradict what we already believe.

Many carpet cleaners believe they are aware of what their customers are willing to pay for a carpet cleaning job.

If you try to show them evidence that customers will pay quite a lot more than they think they will, the person will sometimes resist the idea quite strongly.

As you read through this book, thoughts like these may come up for you. You may strongly disagree, and you may have things that you have heard or things you think are true to back up your opinions.

Now I'm certainly not suggesting you throw out your common sense. But everything in this book has been proven time and time again all over North America.

What I'm suggesting is that you suspend your disbelief and consider the possibility that what you've always thought was possible for you, doesn't even scratch the surface of what really is possible for you.

Finally we come to self-esteem.

The fact is, if you don't think you're worth it, there is just no way you can allow good things to happen to you. This is nothing less than a tragedy, because you will probably be working your tail off to try and make good things happen the whole time!

Here is another one of those challenging ideas that this book is full of:

You already have what you think you deserve

This can be a very hard idea to accept because of the level of responsibility involved. What it's really saying is that how ever good or bad things are right now, things are that way because that's as good or as bad as you will allow them to be.

It also means that you can't change those external circumstances without changing yourself first.

I am in the business of helping people to succeed. I sell them products and services that make their businesses better and make them more money.

I came across a very challenging statement that someone told me once, and it really brought me up short.

This guy said to me, "If your clients were able to make the changes that you are suggesting that they make... they'd already be doing it."

Whoa, hold on here. What this guy was saying is that my clients would have already found a way without my answers if they were really ready to make the changes in their businesses that I suggest.

In a way that is true. However it is also true that people seek out my answers when they are ready for them.

If you are ready to go to the next level in your business, and you are aware that you need some missing information as to how to do it, you will seek out that information. If you are ready for the change when you find it, you'll be able to use that information to make your life and your business better.

That's probably why you are reading this book right now. You are seeking for a way to make things better. If you weren't ready, you probably wouldn't care, and you'd probably decide that you had something better to do.

It has happened that someone has paid good money for my services but has quite literally fought everything that I suggested. Needless to say, we weren't able to make any real improvements in their business.

It is impossible to make massive sweeping positive advancements within a company and not change anything. But people are afraid of change. They are worried that things might get worse... or that it might become very uncomfortable for them.

Human beings are very afraid of the unknown (fear). Why are kids afraid of the dark? The scary thing about the dark is you don't know what's out there, because you can't see!

I bring all of this up because it is underneath your success. It is the reason you will succeed on a massive scale... or you will fail, or you will stay right where you are in spite of everything you try.

If I left this out, I'd be leaving out probably THE most important success concept there is.

You simply cannot operate at a level that is above where you really think and feel that you belong. It won't work, and it will drive you crazy.

To succeed in business, yes you need the tools. You need the systems— but you also have to really feel you deserve it.

If you aren't willing to work on yourself... don't even try to work on your business, because it won't work.

IMPORTANT NOTICE!... REALLY!

Get FREE Stuff!

I have a gift for you to start off our relationship right...

This book talks about a powerful presentation you can use to build value and help you sell your services. You can get your <u>own</u> copy of this presentation **RIGHT NOW** at:

www.offthevan.com/book

Enjoy!

Mark Kennedy

2.
What Does It Take?

First let's define exactly what we're after here.

In order to succeed and be free from all of the 'traps' we've talked about so far, we need at least a level three company that is properly managed and well-structured.

So right off the bat, we know we need to build a company that is bringing in somewhere around a million dollars a year in gross revenue.

We know that we want this thing to operate at a profit margin of 15% or more, so that we're personally bringing in somewhere around $150,000 a year.

We know that we need a general manager that will handle everything, and it's important that this manager handle things according to the systems that we set up, NOT according to the way they personally think things should be done, which is the way most managers behave in this industry.

We have to be able to profitably grow, meaning this business has to be scaleable. We have to be able to pay for this growth as we go. Sure, you might be able to do it if you had $500,000 to invest, but I'm assuming that you don't!

The business has to make enough profit to pay for the growth of the company, meaning that it must pay you, but there must be enough left over so that you can buy the equipment, the advertising, rent the offices, and hire the employees you'll need to grow it.

As it grows, you'll need to be able to keep control of it, meaning you'll need well-structured systems for measurement and accountability so that you'll know exactly where everything stands at all times, even when you're away. You'll need to know that all of the systems within the business are being followed by the employees. You'll need an easy way to check on this.

It's also important that this business not chase you around the room all of the time, meaning it can't destroy your quality of life while you're building it.

Yes, you'll need to work hard... yes, you'll need to make investments of time and money, but your business shouldn't eat you and your family alive in the process!

Maybe most importantly, you'll need a vision for all of this, so that next week or next month when you go to work cleaning carpet, you'll know exactly what you're building and how it will all work. This will give you hope, but it won't be based on nothing.

Your hope will be based on a solid plan of action.

You can realize this goal.

You can do it with systems in three areas.

1. The Sales System
2. The Marketing System
3. The Management System

1. The Sales System—

The profitability of your company overall is addressed by a system of sales that will instantly increase the amount of money you make from every job you do. This money will allow you to buy your way out of the traps and build your business.

In addition it will build customer loyalty and increase customer retention, and allow you to charge almost whatever you want.

This is the system I used to charge clients $50,000 for. They paid it because it could double the profit they were making from their business in 28 days.

2. The Marketing System—

This is a proven system of promoting your business based on what works today. There are really only a few things you need to do to profitably grow your business. (Less than ten)

This system keeps the new customers coming in, and keeps the old customers coming back for more.

Each time a customer calls to do business with you, the sales system makes sure you make as much money as you possibly can from them, and it reinforces the relationship between the customers and your company so that they keep coming back.

Together, these two systems allow you to grow and make money doing it.

3. The Management System—

This system allows you to control it all. This is the system that will allow you to grow without losing your mind in the process.

This allows you to hire people and manage them effectively. It includes pay structures that are performance-based, so that when people act in their own selfish interest, they inadvertently act in your best interest as well.

This system allows your business to run on it's own and you will have clear accountability for every employee in every position.

Your growth is clearly laid out, from a level one company, to a profitable level two, to a level three company that accomplishes all of the goals we've been talking about.

This system lets you grow without the insanity and chaos, which are the reasons that most small business owners don't want to grow.

Focusing on these three areas will allow you to build a strong, healthy, business that achieves all of your goals, gives you profit and freedom, and doesn't ruin your life in the process.

Before we get into exactly how these three systems can completely turn your business life around, let's talk about some concepts that are behind the very structure of this.

3.
Concepts Behind the Systems

These concepts are really leverage points that you can use to your advantage that will allow you to massively succeed in ways you aren't right now.

The first is about how you can grow a business.

There are really only three ways you can grow a business.

That's it.

Three.

The three ways are:

1. **Do business with more customers**
2. **Do more business with each customer when you do business with them**
3. **Do business with them more frequently**

Let's examine these and see how they apply to you and what you want to do.

1. Do business with more customers

Everyone seems to be trying to do this. It's the most obvious one. It's no coincidence that all of the carpet cleaning business success gurus are selling 'marketing' as the magical cure for everything that's wrong with your business.

The logic behind this one goes like this:

> If you have 100 customers and you are making a certain amount of money, and you want to make twice as much money, then <u>you need twice as many customers</u> in order to do it.

So, you market, and you grow, and you make more money.

This works, it's effective, and it's certainly one of the things we have to use in order to build our million-dollar, level three company.

2. Do more business with each customer when you do business with them

Very few people ever think of this one, and yet it is one of the most powerful of the three.

Why? Simply because you don't need more customers to make it work.

It works like this:

> If you have 100 customers and you are making a certain amount of money and you want to make twice as much money, then you need to sell <u>twice as much to each customer</u> in order to do it.

If you think about this, it has some interesting and very powerful advantages, as well as one huge disadvantage.

First of all, it's immediate... you get the results right away.

As soon as you start selling twice as much to each customer, you are instantly as profitable as the person that doubled the size of his business through marketing.

The difference is time. If you have 100 customers right now, it's taken you a certain amount of time to get them. For someone to double the size of their customer base, it's going to take time, and while they're doing it, they're going to have to pay for marketing.

Marketing is expensive. In fact, it would be very easy to eat up all of the profit from the new customers while they were marketing for more.

What this means is that for someone to double the size of their customer base, they are probably going to be spending a bunch of money and not really making much extra from it until they stop marketing.

The disadvantage of this approach is that you have to be able to sell each customer twice as much... the customers are going to have an opinion about that, and it might not be a good one!

Maybe the customers just won't buy twice as much, or maybe they can't afford to spend twice as much.

Maybe if you try to sell them twice as much, they will take their business elsewhere. Now you've lost a customer and so not only have you failed to get the additional money, but you've lost the original money as well!

3. Do business with them more frequently

This is another powerful way to grow your business. The logic behind this one goes something like this:

> If you have 100 customers and you are making a certain amount of money, and you want to make twice as much money, then you <u>get your customers to buy twice as often</u> in order to do it.

This one is obvious. It also explains the power of marketing to your own database. If you can keep a customer coming back, as frequently as possible, you can make more money from that customer than someone else who is lax about it can.

Now I want you to please realize that I've used these examples as just that... examples. I completely oversimplified them to make a point.

But there is one final point I want to make.

In these examples, we talked about making twice the money using each method individually. But what would happen if we used them all at once?

If we used all three methods together, the effects of each one would be **multiplied by the effects of the other two!**

What does this really mean? Well, if we truly could get twice the number of customers by using principle #1, and sell each of those customers twice as much using principle #2, and get each of those customers to come back twice as often using principle #3... all at the same time... we'd make EIGHT TIMES THE MONEY!

That's the kind of result that's exciting. Think about it. We start off with a business that has 100 customers and is making a certain amount of money.

We double the number of customers, get them to buy more, and get them to come back more frequently and... All of a sudden we are making EIGHT TIMES the money we were before!

Because the results of what we're doing multiply back on themselves.

How does this all relate? Well, the sales system primarily makes you money through principle number two. It can make you quite a bit more money from your current customers than you are right now, and because it really builds value, it keeps them loyal and coming back for more.

The marketing system gets new customers and allows you to multiply the effect of the sales system by using it with more people. It also keeps your current customers coming back more frequently than they would have, so it maximizes principle number 3.

This works the other way too, however. For instance, let's assume that we've done exactly what I just said. You're now making eight times what you were before, life is good.

But you get complacent– you get lazy.

And you let one of the three slip.

What happens?

Instantly, you divide the results you're getting by 2, meaning that instead of making eight times what you were, now you're only making four times... literally half of what you were making when things were good.

It happens all the time.

And that's why you absolutely need the management system, because it keeps you on track. Without it, I can absolutely guarantee things will fall back to the way they were.

The sales system and the marketing system are the systems that actually make you the increased money. They cause your business to grow and produce more profit than before.

For that reason, they are sexy. They make money. But the management system is the structure behind it all. It's what keeps everything happening, without it, nothing will last.

Now unfortunately I suppose I have to qualify something. It's a crazy world out there and if I don't do this, someone out there is going to call up and complain because they only made six times the amount of money... or seven times... or five times, instead of eight!

I am using 100 customers and two times the results for each system to make a point.

What I want you to understand is the principle behind this. If you do all three, the result multiplies and is many times more powerful than doing one alone.

That marketing package you bought? It might be great, but alone, it could only produce a result that is two times where you are now. If you do all of these together, you'll get to multiply even those incredible results times two… and then multiply times two again! That's the point. Not exactly, but in principle.

So I can almost guarantee you that you won't make eight times more money, but if you do it all, you can minimize the effects of commercial work that can't be up-sold, houses where the owner isn't home and can't be contacted, people standing you up for appointments, you get the idea.

4.

Understanding Profit And How To Make More Of It

I have shared this formula with countless carpet cleaning business owners, boards of directors of major national franchise organizations, equipment manufacturing companies, real estate and financial companies... the list goes on and on.

In every case, when they really understood the power of this simple formula, they were amazed and quickly realized the truth of it and how they could use it to make more money.

Now I want you to have that same experience...

The formula states that the profit that you make as a company, (Company Profit) is equal to the profit you make on each job, (Profit Per Job) times the number of jobs.

(Company Profit) = (Profit Per Job) X (Number Of Jobs)

Now at first glance, this simple little formula seems rather obvious and simple, but the real power behind it can be seen when you start messing with it.

Let's assume we want to double the amount of profit we make in a year.

If we go crazy with a marketing campaign and we double the number of jobs, as you can plainly see, we'd make twice the profit.

The disadvantage of this approach we've already talked about. Massive marketing campaigns are expensive and they tend to eat up profit, so the profit per job is less.

It also takes a lot of time to double the customer base.

The other way to make double the money, is to double the profit per job.

For us to make twice the money on each job, we'd have to double the price, right?

Well, actually... No.

Let's put some numbers to this so you can see how it really works.

Let's say that you own a company with one van and you did 20 jobs in a one-week period.

The average size of each job was $200, you did 20 jobs, so your total income for the week was $4,000.

Let's say you make a 20% profit margin on the work you do. (If you're running a one-van company, you'll probably argue that you really make much more than that, but we'll talk about that next, so play along with me here...)

To fit this into the formula, what we'd say is that on each $200 job, we made 20% which is $40.

So the formula looks like this:

(Company Profit) = (Profit Per Job) X (Number Of Jobs)

$$\$800 = \$40 \text{ (per job)} \times 20 \text{ (jobs)}$$

Now, if we wanted to double the company profit, we COULD double the number of jobs we do...

The problem with this approach is that we'd need twice as many customers, and we'd need another van. We'd also need another employee. Basically we'd need to double the size of our company.

However, if we could double the profit per job, then we could also make twice the money.

That would look like this:

(Company Profit) = (Profit Per Job) X (Number Of Jobs)

$1600 = $80 (per job) X 20 (jobs)

Here is what you have to understand— In order to double the profit per job, we don't have to double the price. We have to raise the price... yes... but only by $40.

If we could raise the price of our average job by just $40, so that the new average job size was $240, we'd make twice the money we were before!

Why is this true?

Think about it like this— If our average job size was $200 and we are making a 20% profit margin, that means that we are making $40 per job in profit—

But it also means that our cost for that job is $160. If we raise the price by $40, does our cost increase? The answer is no. Our costs on the job are things like labor, machinery, chemicals, insurance, advertising, etc.

But what we charge isn't really related to any of those things. If we raise the price, we can literally make twice the money, and we can do it immediately! We don't have to wait, and there is no marketing expense. We don't have to buy another van, we don't need twice the customers… but we still make twice the money!

It would be like running an airline. Let's say you run an airline and the planes each seat 100 people.

When you sell 80 seats in a plane, you cover all your expenses. You've paid for your gas, your pilots, all the ground crew, ticket agencies… everyone and everything you need to pay is paid for when you sell 80 seats in a plane.

Let's say you're flying your planes with 85 seats filled, so you're making pure profit for those five seats. (80 seats pays for expenses + 5 seats is profit)

Trying to grow your carpet cleaning business by marketing alone would be like buying more planes so you could make more money off of five seats sold in each one of those new planes.

But what you really ought to do is sell the remaining 15 seats in the planes you already have, because those seats are pure 100% profit!

This principle works… whether you're running an airline, selling chemicals, or selling carpet cleaning services.

Once your expenses are paid, anything else you add on to the job, falls to the bottom line as profit.

Let's talk about the holes in this theory. First of all, let's deal with the big one. How do you think your customers are going to feel about you raising prices?

Let's also be real about this— Many carpet cleaners claim that they could raise their prices, but then they don't.

People charge what they think they can.

Maybe they charge what they think they deserve. But when you talk about raising prices, it scares people. It brings up fear at a very deep level.

Many will say, "Sure, I'll raise prices _____ (fill in the blank with next week, next month, or next year...) People love to run down the timeline when they don't want to do something right now.

So what can we do? Well, there is more than one way to raise prices...

We could sell other services for instance.

Obviously if we sell more work, we have to actually DO that work, and our costs go up accordingly.

But what if we could sell something with almost no cost associated with it? If we could do that, then we'd effectively raise the price, without raising the price.

Now let's make it really interesting...

What if we could do both?

What if we could raise prices, without losing our customers, AND we could sell each customer more stuff?

Once again, we double, and then multiply, our results.

5.
How Should You Pay Yourself?

This might seem like an odd topic to find right here in this section of this book, but I think it needs addressing.

One of the big problems faced by owner/operators as they decide to grow is the fact that they look at the world differently than more 'regular' business owners.

In fact, there is a pretty good chance that you've already experienced this as you've read this far in the book.

When I talked about profit margins being 15% or 20%, there is a pretty good chance that if you are a small owner-operator, that you said to yourself, "that doesn't apply to me".

If you said that to yourself, or if you wondered what I was talking about, or why the amount you got to keep was only 15% or 20% in my examples, I'm going to tell you why right now.

For those owners of larger carpet cleaning businesses that might be reading this, they'll know exactly what I mean when I talk about a profit margin in the realm of 15% to 20% and this is exactly the problem that I want to address here.

If you are an owner/operator, one of the things that is probably keeping you trapped at your current level, is your own viewpoint.

What I mean by this is that as long as you continue to look at the money that you bring in as what you make, you will be unable to grow.

This viewpoint seems to happen at two levels.

First is the carpet cleaner who does a job for a person on a certain afternoon for $400 and then proudly says, "I just made $400 this afternoon!"

If you ask them how much money they made last year, they will tell you how much gross, total revenue they brought in! "I made $70,000 last year!" But they never seem to have any money!

This is the most unbusinesslike of the viewpoints.

This cleaner actually isn't taking into account ANY expenses at all. He is literally thinking that the entire $400 is his to keep. ("Come on honey... let's go out to dinner!")

Now anyone knows that there are expenses associated with doing that job.

There are chemical costs, fuel costs, wear and tear on the machinery, not to mention the owner's time, and the cost to sell or market in order to get that job.

The point I'm making here is that even though absolutely everyone admits that these costs are real... Many owner/operators will take the money and spend it, and not take those expenses into account. Then when it's time to pay a supplier, or a bill, they will just pay that, and so on.

They will not set aside part of the $400 to pay these bills... rather, they will just pay the bills when they come due.

This absolutely WILL lead to problems, because it means that they are not being realistic about what they are making.

The next level of thinking, which is only slightly more elevated than the first, is the person who realizes that as an owner/operator, he has expenses, that may be as high as 50%.

This person, when they finish doing the $400 job, will realize that they just made $200. They may or may not set the other $200 aside for expenses, but at least they are much more accurate about what they are making.

Why is this important?

This is important because it makes it very hard to ever grow.

Think about it. If you think you are making all the money... or you think you are making 50% of the money, what happens when you decide to hire someone?

You have to pay them out of your pocket!

You literally have to take the 100% or the 50% that you think you are making, and pay this employee out of that.

Expenses generally rise to meet income.

What that means is that your life is probably set up so that you need all of the money you are making right now.

So it becomes completely impossible to pay anyone else out of the money you already need to live on.

Now many business owners struggle through this, but it is a problem of viewpoint. There is a much better way of looking at it, and when you look at your business another way, it becomes much easier to grow.

The New Viewpoint That Will Make ALL The Difference!

Alright, so here it is: When you start out in business, you really have two roles. You are an owner/operator. Or maybe it would be more accurate to say that you are an owner/technician.

You should get paid two ways as well.

What I'm saying here, is that you should get paid as an owner.

You should also get paid as a technician.

The second you do this, you immediately have a new viewpoint about your business, and it is a much more business-like viewpoint than the one you probably had before.

So let's look at this.

What I'm suggesting here is that you adopt a pay structure that you would pay for any technician, and as long as you do the work, you pay yourself the same amount that any technician would make.

In addition to that, after you pay all your expenses, AND YOU PAY THE TECHNICIAN, WHOEVER THAT IS, if there is anything left over, you take it as owner's pay.

However, and this is important: You cannot take more than 15% of the Total Revenue, even if it is there to take. In fact, the goal is to leave some money in the business so that you can invest in the business and market and grow.

What this does from a practical standpoint is, it separates you from the business.

You need to do a couple of other things as well. You need a separate business account.

Think about what this will do for you.

You get to see the money coming in as a technician would. But you also get to see in a very real way, how much you are making as an owner.

Now I'm not going to lie to you here, the result of this might be very depressing at first.

If it is, that's good… because it means that your business needs work. And it almost certainly does… and I'm guessing that you almost certainly know it!

And the point of all of this is that you absolutely DO need to do something different in order to really succeed.

Or I guess you could keep your head stuck in the sand.

But if you do that, you're not going to get anywhere.

The power of this is that it allows you to see where you'd be if you hired a technician (replacing yourself) and operated as an owner.

Now obviously you're almost certainly not going to be able to live on 15% of what one technician can produce, so you're probably going to have to get a job in order to supplement your business-owner income. (What if you got a job as a part-time technician, working for your own company?)

I hope you're beginning to get my point here. This method of operation will allow you to see the real impact of hiring new people from the standpoint of a business owner.

It will also allow you to pay yourself what you really should for the work you are doing in your business.

Now I've seen people take this and run with it in a bad way. They've decided that they were worth $60,000 a year because that's what a 'marketing' person would be worth, and so they justified taking more money than they should out of the business because they were doing some marketing.

The fact is, if you were an owner, running a business that brought in $200,000 a year total, and you were keeping 15%– in other words, a whopping $30,000 for your efforts... you'd never hire a 'marketing' person for $60,000 a year. You couldn't afford it. You'd have to do the marketing yourself. And you'd do the marketing for the $30,000 you were already making. That's just the way it is.

That's how you have to look at it.

This is the reality of the business world. I see so many people refusing to see it... or they hide from the reality of their own situations because they don't want to deal with the unpleasantness of <u>what really is</u>.

They don't want to hear it.

As long as these people refuse to deal with reality, they will remain victims of their own 'traps'. They could get free, but in order to do that, they'd have to deal with a reality that is unpleasant and uncomfortable.

They'd rather lie to themselves than do it.

I can't help them.

No one can.

I hope you're beginning to see why, in order to be really free, and have any hope of financial freedom, a million-dollar, level three company, is necessary.

When I first tell people that, they don't believe it. They think that having a million-dollar company is a luxury... a needless extravagance. They're thinking that if they had a million-dollar company that they'd be rolling in the dough!

Well, not exactly. If you own and run a million-dollar business, and you keep 15%, you'll bring in $150,000 a year. If it's you and your wife, that's the equivalent of making $75,000 each. You'll probably be comfortable... But I wouldn't say you were 'rich'.

If you have kids that you want to send to college, that's going to cost some money, and you'll need some retirement, so you're going to have to save some of that.

All in all, this isn't crazy... it's practical, it will work. It's what it takes these days to make a decent life for yourself.

At this level, you'll be able to take some vacations, you'll be able to see some of the world. You'll be able to donate to causes you think are worthy...

And if things slow down, and your business takes a downturn because of a slow economy or something else, well maybe you're making 15% of $800,000 instead of $1,000,000– so you're making $120,000 instead of $150,000... but you're not going to starve!

If you set your business up with the right systems in place so that it can run without your constant and never-ending supervision, you'll be able to keep it indefinitely, even as you grow older and aren't able to do hard physical work for 50 to 60 hours a week.

You'll also be able to sell it if you ever want to or need to, and it will be worth as much as it possibly can. If you bought a commercial building and let the business rent space from you, you'll have that as well.

All in all, you'll probably be in pretty good shape.

Or, you could continue on as you are now and hope that things get better. You could pat yourself on the back and tell yourself you're making more money than you really are, and you can tell yourself that you're building something that you can sell for top dollar, even though there is no way it can run without you.

The choice is yours. What I'm offering is a more sensible approach to this thing... A way that makes sense. And it's necessary if you're going to spend your life doing this, it really is.

Mine isn't the only answer... but it's a pretty good one!

Let's explore each of the systems so you'll know how, and why they work, as well as exactly what they'll do for you.

First though, let's look at exactly what it is you need out of these systems in order to accomplish your goals:

- **Greater Profit–** You're going to need money in order to build your business. You're going to need it to be able to hire, to pay employees, to pay for marketing, to buy equipment, and ultimately to reward yourself for all of your hard work in putting this together.

- **Better Customer Retention—** It costs so much to get a new customer... there is no way you can let them go because of lack of attention. Also, if you're going to charge customers more than the barest minimum, you have to be able to justify that. You can't lose your customers while you're in the process of making money.

- **Competitive Advantage—** You have to be able to give your customers valid, good, strong, clear-cut reasons why doing business with you is the only choice that makes any sense.

- **Profitable Growth—** You've got to grow a business, and you're going to need to be able to pay for that growth as you go. Again, if you won the lottery and could pour unlimited funds into your business, yes, you could make it work, but you need a more likely plan than that.

- **Control And Freedom—** Your business can't chase you around the room. Yes, you're going to have to work at it, and you're going to have to work hard. But you should know that the work won't last forever, and you should be able to be certain that you are building a situation that will free you, instead of imprison you.

- **Ability To Be Free From The Business—** Ultimately you should be able to keep it, sell it, give it to your kids... whatever you decide. You need options. The thing can't depend on you in order to run.

- **Meet The Initial Goals You Had When You Started It—** The business needs to be a vehicle that provides you with the type of life that you want. You started a business so that it could support you, and your business needs to do that.

6.

What It Takes To Build A Company That Is Worth Something And Gets You Free

The Sales System

For the sales system to do it's part in getting you free, it has to do a few things.

• It has to sell more. It has to make you more money from the customers you're already dealing with.

• It must justify the new, higher prices. These prices are higher because you will raise them, but also because you will be selling more services and when you do this, you don't want to lose your customers.

• Here's an important one- The sales system has to be able to be used by a typical carpet cleaning technician. In other words, you shouldn't have to be a trained psychologist to be able to use it… it should be simple and straightforward. It's got to be usable by the kind of person you are likely to hire.

• It must be ethical. It can't rely on bait and switch tactics or anything like that.

• It can't feel like a 'shell game' to the customer.

• The customers should never feel like they're being 'sold'.

- You and your technicians shouldn't feel like you are pressuring the customers.

- It should make your work life easier.

- It should completely win over your customers, educating them so that they wouldn't dream of using anyone other than you.

- It should provide a level of consistency throughout your company.

That's a pretty tall order, but the sales system does exactly that.

The sales system is the system I sold to several very large companies when I first started out as a consultant. I charged these companies over $50,000 for this system because it did all of these things.

Not only that, but it added between $50 and $100 of pure profit to the bottom line on EVERY JOB THEY DID!

Think about that...

That's as much as $200 to $400 each day per van!

In a week, that's $1,000 to $2,000 per van.

In a month, $4,000 to $8,000

In a year, $50,000 to $100,000

...And then remember that's PER VAN!

Some of these companies run anywhere from 10 to 50 vans...

You do the math!

This system literally doubled the amount of profit these massive companies made.

Many of them made several hundred thousand dollars each year of additional money as a result of this system.

A few of them made millions

And it all started within about 28 days.

Not many consultants could come in and make that kind of difference that fast, but I was able to, using this system.

You can do the exact same thing yourself in your own company.

DISCLAIMER: Obviously these were well-run companies that completely implemented everything. There is no guarantee of performance or results with this system. Your actual performance could be more or less than this.

Concepts

I've spent a lot of time showing you how critical price is in making money for your company.

You've seen how after a certain point, (when you have your expenses paid) anything after that largely falls to the bottom line and you get to keep it.

We also discussed raising prices two ways, just outright charging more, and also selling more items to each customer.

Sometimes, people will question how necessary it is to have a sales system. If you think about it, how much more powerful would it be to have a pre-designed system that predictably guides the customer to buying more?

The only other option is to just have people show up and wing it.

Now maybe you, as the owner, are pretty good at that, but what about your employees, current and future?

Even a good salesman will have 'off' days.

The only real unanswered question is: How do you get your customers to pay higher prices?

First of all, no one is going to pay more, unless you give them a reason to... and, by the way, it had better be a very good one!

Most carpet cleaners don't really understand this simple fact, and of the ones that do... most are really bad at applying it.

As if that weren't bad enough, almost no one has any idea of how to get their employees to buy into this and do it!

How to do this can probably best be illustrated with a story.

Winning Over Your Customers By Telling Them How You Make Beer

In the 1970's, there was a famous brewing company that had a problem: They wanted to be number one in sales and they weren't!

They were more like number ten.

They had tried everything they could think of, but nothing seemed to work.

They tried different advertising agencies, different media, different creative teams. Finally, they had worked their way through most of the large national advertising firms, and all they had to show for it was a bunch of frustration.

Finally in desperation they called in a very well-known, well-respected, and high-priced guru.

The man met them in the board room of their main office in Milwaukee and they told him about their problem.

They reached an agreement and decided to work together and then they told him that they'd like to give him a tour of their brewery which was located on the shore of Lake Michigan.

The tour guide started the tour by explaining that they got all the water for their brewing process from three wells that were drilled over 300 feet deep into the bedrock.

The advertising guru asked why they would go to so much trouble to drill for water when they had one of the largest fresh bodies of water in the world, (Lake Michigan) right there on their doorstep?

The tour guide explained how the mineral content of the water at that depth was perfect for making beer, and how if they used surface water, it would affect the taste of the beer.

Later on in the tour the guide showed the group the sterilization room where they used live steam at over 350° to sterilize all of the containers, the tubing, the vats, and the bottles to prevent contamination. He explained that even a small amount of bacteria would contaminate an entire batch.

Further on in the tour, the advertising man was surprised to be shown a fully stocked laboratory.

"This", explained the tour guide, "is where we developed the mother yeast cell."

"What's a mother yeast cell?" asked the advertising man.

The tour guide explained how they had done over 1,100 experiments to develop the perfect yeast for brewing beer, and that all of the yeast used in their brewing process was a descendant of the one mother yeast cell they developed right there in their own lab.

At the end of the tour, the guide showed the group the bottled, finished product. He showed them how the master brewers would randomly select bottles from the line and test them for pH and taste and explained that sometimes entire batches would be rejected for subtle variations in taste... stuff that we probably wouldn't even notice!

At the end of the tour the advertising man turned to the board of directors and said, "Gentlemen... I have your answer! Let's go back to the boardroom."

They all went back to the boardroom and the advertising man looked at them carefully and said, "I have one question for you. Why is it that you don't tell people what you do here?"

The men looked at each other and finally one of them spoke up and said, "But that's the way EVERYONE does it... if you went to any major brewery in the country, you'd basically see the same things we have here."

The advertising man smiled and said, "That may very well be, but the American public doesn't know that.

If you tell them, you are going to be perceived, rightly or wrongly, as the only people that do it that way.

If the other breweries do the same thing, they will be perceived as copying you!"

The men on the board looked at each other… After all, they had tried everything else. Maybe this advertising genius was right.

They launched a campaign based on telling people how they made beer. Within the following year, they became the second-best selling beer in the country…

So, how does this apply to you?

Well, let's think about what happens to the average customer when they have their carpets cleaned.

Many times, the customer is responding to some ad or coupon in the mail. If the customer is a referred customer, they may call and ask for a bid.

Most companies just give a price over the phone based on the number of rooms the customer has. The company has to explain that they'll measure everything up when they get there etc.

When the technician arrives at the house, he takes a look at the carpet and gives the customer a price and usually attempts to up-sell the customer. The customer may say 'yes', or they may say 'no'.

Either way, the 'sales presentation' is usually a guy that comes in, looks around, kicks the carpet with the toe of his tennis shoe, and says, "Eighty bucks."

The problem with this approach is obvious.

The customer has an idea in their head about what carpet cleaning is worth, usually based on what they've heard and on the coupons that they see in their mailbox.

The customer has no idea that the coupons are a scam and a rip-off, they think they are real.

So they feel like they know what 'carpet cleaning' is worth, and they pretty much feel like it's all the same.

You hear it in their language. They say things like, "We were thinking of maybe having you do it… or we might just rent a machine and do it ourselves."

This customer really thinks that the rented machine, and the job you will do are all the same.

In other words, carpet cleaning has been reduced to a commodity.

If I want to buy a car, or a computer, or anything else like that, I'm probably going to follow a pretty specific chain of events to do it.

Let's say I want to buy a car.

First I'm going to research it and decide which one I want. Once I've decided which make, which model, and which options I want, I'm now going to try to find it for the best price I can.

I don't want to be taken advantage of, and I've heard that can happen, so I start the process of 'shopping around'.

I might visit various dealerships, I might call, I might use the internet. But somehow, I will get a price on the exact car I want, from all of the dealerships in my area. I might even go out of state.

Finally, one of the dealerships will agree to give me the car for less than any of the others, and I'll go buy the thing.

This works.

I got the deal I wanted… and it works because the car is the same… it's a commodity.

But that's definitely not true with a service. Especially not carpet cleaning.

With carpet cleaning, some people do an incredible job, but most people do a lousy job. Now you know this, but your customer probably doesn't. Educating them about the way this really works is one of the greatest and most powerful sales techniques there is.

What do you suppose would happen if we followed the Brewing Company's example and really told our story.

What if we had a presentation, complete with pictures that showed each and every customer exactly how we make beer? (How we clean carpet.)

What if this presentation pointed out that by following the proper procedure, we could be certain not to void the carpet's warranty?

What if we talked about our guarantee, and let them know that we followed all of the steps in their manufacturer's recommended cleaning process?

What if we showed them all of the steps for the absolute best carpet cleaning that money could buy?

And then charged them for it.

Do you really think there is any way that someone is going to come in and kick their toe on the carpet and take that customer away from you, at any price?

If that customer cares about their home and furnishings at all, they will find a way to use your services.

Why?

Because you gave them several clear-cut reasons to, that's why. They are no longer buying the same thing from several different sources.

Do you think your competitors are using a professional presentation? Most of them probably look like they slept under a bridge last night.

What's great about this is that it doesn't even matter if your competition is providing the same level of service that you are. If they fail to talk about it, there is no way for the customer to know about it.

If they're asleep and lazy… you can take their inaction straight to the bank! And almost all of them are… I guarantee it!

If someone else in your market area is using this system, then together, you will raise the bar and you'll both succeed at capturing the higher end market in your town.

I'm not talking about working for just the Über-rich, I'm talking about your typical middle to upper-middle-class customer that needs their carpets cleaned.

This flat-out works!

It is the first part of the key for you to be able to charge what you need to in order to really make money.

Most people in this industry base their prices, at least in part, on what the competition is doing, and then they try to find a way to make money in spite of that.

This leads to people either doing work they aren't proud of, but they cut the corners because they have to make money...

Or, they do an incredible job, and basically go broke in the process.

You can't price that way and succeed.

You also might think that you're charging a lot and you really might not be. You've got to remember that everything is based on your perception. What might be a huge amount to you might be a small amount to someone else.

What you have to do is to claim the higher ground... and then use the lack of professionalism in this industry to be your best friend, but you can only do that if you can clearly show each and every person you do business with, exactly what they are getting from you that they can't get anywhere else.

If the other companies in your town choose to be horrible at communicating with their customers, we'll let them... after all, that's their choice. But YOU can use it to make a ton of money.

This is a huge opportunity for you.

By the way, the presentation is a very simple two-page affair that ANY carpet-cleaning technician can use. They just point to the pictures and tell the customer what's going on and why it's important, in fact this presentation is being used by hundreds of carpet-cleaning EMPLOYEES all across the country right now.

Part of the system is a pay structure that allows a good technician to earn anywhere from $40,000 to $70,000 a year.

Yes, you read that right, that's not a typo. I've had technicians earn over $70,000 on this system.

That's a 25-year-old employee with a high-school education. Do you think that employee is ever going to leave? Do you think he can find ANYTHING even close to that? No, he can't.

He can raise a family on it though. He can pay for a decent quality of life.

What would THAT do for your employee problems? You'd practically have them beating your door down to come to work for you!

Needless to say, the companies that employ these technicians make much more than that.

So, the first thing we have to do with absolutely everyone we come in contact with is tell our story. But there's something else we can do that is much more powerful even than that!

The field of psychology is an interesting one. It's the study of people and what makes them tick.

Sales psychologists study why people buy and what makes them respond.

Believe it or not, there are actually ways that a person can exert a tremendous amount of influence over another person, without them feeling pressured at all. It's completely sub-conscious.

Large multi-national corporations hire sales psychologists to design their sales models for them.

The psychologists come in and, based on what makes people respond, they design methods of selling that make these corporations millions of dollars of profit.

These techniques are used on you all the time, because they work, and because you don't realize it.

So here's a question: What would happen if YOU could use some of these same techniques in your own company?

If you did, sales would definitely increase.

When I mention this idea to most carpet cleaners I usually get two reactions:

- First, people aren't sure it will work for them, after all they often don't even have a sales force, much less a highly-trained group of people that could use psychology on other people to get them to buy!
- Second, they are concerned about the ethics of it all. Is it right to use psychology-based techniques that create an unconscious response?

While you do need some knowledge of psychology to be able to design the sales model, you don't need more than a basic understanding in order to use it!

The very best sales models are completely built-in to the way that the company does business, so that the actual psychology is pretty much invisible to the employees as well.

Many of the employees may not know exactly why things are done a certain way, they only know that is the way it is supposed to be done at that particular company, so they do it that way.

You can easily do the same thing in your company. You can remove obstacles that unconsciously prevent customers from buying and literally set them up to buy more and they'll never see it!

You can use this to make them happier and more satisfied with their purchases. They'll be more loyal, they'll be more satisfied, AND they'll spend more money! It just couldn't get any better than that!

But what about the ethics of using psychology-based manipulation on your customers. If you have a question about that, that's good... it means you care about ethics and how your customers are treated.

There is no question that if you use unconscious techniques of persuasion to get people to do things that help you, but harm them, that is absolutely wrong.

But what if you used your techniques to actually help them to get a result that they wanted and prevented them from doing business with unethical people that would take advantage of them if they could?

If you had to boil down my concept of how to succeed in this business to a couple of sentences, it would be this:

You have to absolutely provide the best quality of service and level of experience possible... then you have to charge for it and find ways to sell it and market it, because that really is what everyone is looking for.

Everyone wants the best. They may not all be able to afford it, and so everyone may not buy it... but everyone wants the very best.

You are going to stand behind your work... You're going to guarantee their complete satisfaction. You're going to do the work right, and you're going to do them the favor of charging enough so that you don't have to hurry through it.

Not only that, but when they need you again next year, you're going to still be in business, because you won't have gone broke!

Or they could do business with some guy who looks like he slept under a bridge last night, who isn't honest, and who will rip them off if he gets a chance.

He won't take the time he needs to really do a good job, because he isn't charging enough to be able to… He probably isn't trained, he probably doesn't have the equipment that you do, and if he has employees, they probably all look like carnival workers!

The biggest favor you could possibly do for this customer is to convince them to use YOU! No one loses if that happens. You aren't being unethical… you're guiding the customer to make the right choice, the choice they would make if they knew all the facts.

The Psychology Behind The System

There are five main principles we can use to influence our customers. They are:

1. **Strategic Comparison**
2. **Strategic Compromise**
3. **Create Obligation**
4. **Credibility Disclosure**
5. **Use Packages To Change The Base Of The Decision**

Let's talk about each one of these and then we'll talk about how the system is structured to use them all at once!

1. Strategic Comparison– People think by making comparisons.

It's how we all make sense of the world. What's interesting is that we can't stop doing this… It's the way our minds are wired.

This is useful for sales because what it really means is that you can control the perception of something if you can control the things that it gets compared to.

If you show someone the most expensive item in a store, and then let them buy whatever they choose, they will buy more, for a higher price, than if you show them the cheapest items in a store and then let them choose.

The people have the same amount of money, that hasn't changed. What's changed is what they are comparing the item that they finally bought to.

This is common practice in the real estate profession. The agent will often show the customer an overpriced home that is dirty and doesn't show well… and then show them a clean, well-priced home that meets the customers needs.

If the real estate agent had shown the nice home first, the customer probably would have wanted to look around… but after seeing the trashed, overpriced home… the customers can't wait to buy!

So, this principle says that if I sell something, (let's say I sell widgets and I have several different models, ranging in price from $100 to $1,000) I'd be far better off showing my customers the $1,000 widgets first… and then letting them buy whatever they want… as opposed to showing them the $100 widgets and then trying to up-sell them.

In one study that was done by a university, the average sale price nearly doubled as a result of this! So the effect is not small… in fact it's huge!

So this works, and it's powerful.

Now let's think about this…

How do most people sell carpet cleaning?

Most times, they start off by advertising the lowest price they possibly can to get people to call. (In other words, they show them the $100 widget!)

Even if they don't advertise that way, the conversation generally goes something like this:

Carpet cleaner –"It will be $140 to clean the carpet… But we also have this really great protector that will help keep your carpet cleaner and make it last longer, and it's an additional $70.

We also have a deodorizer that we can apply for an additional $40… What do you think?"

Customer – "I think I'll just take the cleaning."

Do you see what the carpet cleaner did? He started at the bottom and tried to work up.

So what that means is that after he put the initial price of $140 out there, every price from then on was perceived as being high by comparison!

Because it was!

Now look at another way we could do it–

Carpet cleaner –"It will be $250 to clean your carpet…
That includes this really great protector that will help keep
your carpet cleaner and make it last longer, and it also
includes a deodorizer.

The cleaning and the protector without the deodorizer
would be $210…

And the cleaning by itself would be $140.

What do you think?"

Customer – "I think I'll take the cleaning and the
protector for $210."

The principle is that we always want to give a high price
first and work down, as opposed to giving a low price first
and trying to work up.

The high price makes all our other prices seems cheaper
by comparison.

The low price makes all our other prices seem higher by
comparison.

This is a simple way that we can alter the customer's
perception of what we're offering, just by slightly changing
the way that we present things.

We can also give them something else that's expensive to
compare the price to. For instance, what if we compared the
cost of cleaning the carpet to the cost of replacement?

How You Can Use It-

Start off by offering your highest priced options first and give them less expensive options after that.

2. Strategic Compromise– What this principle says is that if you ask someone to buy something, and they say 'no', and then you 'give-in' by making them a lesser offer, ... there is tremendous pressure for them to 'give-in' as well.

What is different about it is that it requires you to first get a 'no' from the customer.

I taught this principle to the manager of a rug cleaning plant in New England and he taught it to his little girl...

His daughter was in the sixth grade, and her school was having a raffle. The student who sold the most tickets would win a prize.

The raffle tickets were $1 a piece. The rug plant manager told his daughter to rubber-band ten of the tickets together, and her 'sales presentation' went like this:

She'd walk up to the door, ring the doorbell, and when the 'customer' answered the door, she'd explain the raffle to the 'customer'. She'd then ask them if they'd like to buy ten raffle tickets for $10.

Most of them said, "No".

Then she'd ask them if they'd like to buy just ONE ticket for a dollar!

Most people bought!

Of course she won the contest for selling the most tickets in the whole school!

Now obviously she was using two principles here if you think about it.

First, she gave them an expensive option, so her other option would seem cheap by comparison.

Then, she made them an offer, got them to say no, and then 'gave in' by offering a much smaller offer...

How could they say no?

We can use this by offering an expensive option first, and then letting the customer say no, and then dropping down to a less expensive option.

It works hand-in-hand with the first principle of giving them something expensive to compare things to.

How You Can Use It-

When you give them the most expensive option first, get them to say 'no' and then present a less expensive option.

3. Create Obligation— This principle states that anytime you do something for someone else, especially if you give them some kind of gift, there is a strong tendency to feel like they 'owe you one' on the part of the other person.

You see this when a couple has someone over for dinner. After the dinner, at the doorway, when everyone is saying goodbye, very often the couple that came over for dinner will say, "We'll have to have you over sometime."

This couple feels an obligation to return the favor.

We can use this tendency by giving the customer a gift. Then the customer will feel a sense of obligation to 'pay us back'.

How You Can Use It-

Give the customer a gift <u>BEFORE</u> you give them your sales presentation or a price. Then they can 'pay you back', by giving you the job! The gift that I recommend is a bottle of spotter.

4. Credibility Disclosure– This principle states that anytime you admit a small weakness that the customer wouldn't have known about on their own, they will assume you are honest.

Obviously you know you're honest... The problem is, the customer may not!

Perception is reality. If we control the perception, then we control the reality.

It's pretty important that your customers trust you. And they may already, in fact they probably do. But it never hurts to reinforce something as important as this.

Here's how this works. You have to admit a small flaw, something that isn't critical, but something that the customer wouldn't have known about on their own.

The best way to do this is to find something that won't clean up completely, like a traffic lane, and point it out to them and tell them that it may not completely come out.

This isn't going to be something they want to hear, but it gives you tremendous credibility, because you're telling them something that you really didn't have to. They probably don't think that their carpet is going to look like it did the day they had it installed, but the fact that you're saying it, makes you believable!

How You Can Use It-

Find something that won't clean out completely... a traffic lane, a stain, shading... and call it to the customer's attention. Tell them that you'll be able to get it absolutely clean, but you probably won't be able to completely restore the appearance.

5. Use Packages To Change The Base Of The Decision– By offering different service levels and pricing, you are able to offer something to everyone. Then, people can pick the service level, and the price, that suits them the best.

Most carpet cleaners just give the customer a price, by offering different levels of service you are able to be a little more, all things to all people.

Having the different packages also allows you to use the other principles that we've already talked about.

How You Can Use It-

Have three different service levels and offer the most expensive one first, and work your way down from there. This will allow you to use all the other principles and the customer will feel like they are ordering off of a menu.

Alright, so those are the basic principles behind the sales system. Let's really look at exactly how the system is set up so you can really see exactly how this thing works.

7.

The Structure Of The Sales System

Alright, so we've talked about a lot of principles…

How to grow your business, how to increase profits with price… how to tell our story, and several principles based on psychology that can be used to sell.

Let's talk very specifically about how this system uses all these principles so you can clearly see exactly how this will work in your business.

First of all, you understand that you have three packages, platinum, gold, and silver.

The first package you offer is the most expensive package and it has to be the most expensive option you provide.

The way this thing works in general is that people will usually take the platinum package about 25% of the time. They'll take the gold about 50% of the time, and of course they'll take the silver about 25% of the time.

There is no reason that we can't structure these packages to be advantageous to you. Here is what they look like:

	Platinum	Gold	Silver
Furniture Moving	✔		
Protector	✔	✔	
Cleaning	✔	✔	✔

Think about what this means— If someone wants their furniture moved, that's a platinum package…you are going to have to mess with it. But you're charging them for it, AND they are automatically taking protector as well!

Your most popular package will be the gold package, which also happens to be the easiest and most profitable package you could do!

If you present this right, you will only do silver packages about 25% of the time.

You will be charging a fair (for you) price for furniture moving, so if you get a platinum package, it will be worth doing.

You'll get gold packages most of the time, and the great thing is, you won't be moving furniture but you'll still be selling protector.

If you get a silver package, you'll still be making money because you'll charge enough to make money, but you'll still get the job.

- You'll be moving furniture only about 25% of the time, and getting paid well for it.
- You'll be selling protector about 75% of the time
- You'll maximize every sale without having to pressure or 'sell' the customer
- If you're using a script and you train your people... nearly anyone can be effective at sales

---

A couple of things about this concept.

First of all, the most powerful thing about this is that it sells protector. It also justifies your price, increases customer retention and all of that... but man does it sell protector!

Now many times people will tell me that they sell a lot of protector already. But they can almost never tell me a percentage. They can't give me dollar amounts... all they can do is tell me it's a lot.

Having worked with hundreds of carpet cleaners, I have found that in nearly every case... almost completely without exception, 'a lot' of protector means 30% or less!

Even if it were higher than that, you have to remember, that this is the owner of the company we're talking about. There is no way that person's ever going to be able to hire a whole group of people that can sell it as well as he can!

UNLESS... there is a powerful, well-designed sales system in place.

One client of mine has an average protector sales percentage of over 91%! Their average job size is over $350 and they run 10 crews every day! These are employees doing this... typical carpet cleaning techs.

This sales system increased their average job size from $140 per job to over $350 as soon as it was implemented.

Remember, these were the same vans, the same customers... the ONLY thing that changed was that they started using this system.

My point is, the owner/operator that says that he sells 'a lot' of protector, as if he doesn't need to sell more, is arguing for a trap that will make it impossible for him to ever grow his business or get the maximum performance from it.

He is not only letting himself down, but he is letting down all of the employees that work for him, because every one of them could make more money if this owner would make the decisions that would result in success for the business!

Another point is that many people have tried 'package selling' in this industry. Most of them have had very little success with it. This is because the packages without the psychology, don't work.

The packages without the psychology... don't work!

This has been proven time and time again. The packages have to be presented in the right way or the customer will actually be unconsciously 'pushed' to buy the cheapest one.

This isn't hard to do... again, you don't have to be a trained psychologist to use this system, you simply have to make sure that your people use it as designed and it works! It's that easy.

One other final note: People that have been moving furniture as part of their service since the beginning of time, often find it hard to conceive that their customers would ever settle for not having everything moved!

This is a classic case of making a decision based on your own perceptions and then fighting to justify it.

The truth is, about 25% of the time, you WILL be moving furniture, except that if you're going to mess with that… (huge liability, takes LOTS of time…) you're going to charge for it, AND you're going to sell protector as well.

If you ask anyone if they'd like something done for free, or for nearly free, they will almost always say yes. But this isn't fair for you or your technicians.

We get around this by showing the customer how we'll be cleaning all of the visible carpet. If you can see it, we'll clean it! Obviously this means we will have to move some light furniture such as coffee tables, dining room chairs, etc., but it will get us out of moving the sleeper sofas most of the time.

We're definitely NOT saying we won't move furniture, we're just not going to do it for free anymore. (Or like some cleaners, who charge a ridiculously low price… something like 0.04¢ a square foot for it)

We have an option that includes furniture moving, and if they want it, we'll be happy to do it, but we've got to make money at it or we won't survive as a business.

The system contains scripts that tell you exactly what to say to keep your customers happy even though you've changed things.

The best approach is honesty. Remember the principle of the credibility disclosure? Simply tell your customers that you've changed things around to give your customers more choices and that furniture moving is VERY time-consuming, so you've had to charge something for it. (Or, you've had to charge more for it!)

Carpet cleaners are often absolutely terrified of telling their customers anything that they might not want to hear. In general, people are reasonable as long as you are. If your customers are unreasonable, get rid of them... they'll ruin your life!

Components Of The Sales System

In order to make this system work, it has to be well-defined. That's why every one of these packages contains franchise-grade systems.

The sales systems contains scripts for the technicians and the person answering the phone. The person answering the phone actually is in a very powerful selling position, especially since absolutely every customer has to talk to them in order to book a job.

However, scripts won't do you any good if your people won't or can't learn them. For that reason, I've included something called a calibration sheet to go along with each script.

A calibration sheet is a way of scoring the performance of a CSR (Customer Service Representative–the person who answers the phone) or a technician that is using a script.

Each critical area of the script is scored, while the CSR or technician gives the script in a role-play environment. When they are done, the score is reviewed. This does two things. First, it gives the CSR or technician instant feedback as to how well they used the script. The specific areas they missed can easily be reviewed with them.

However, other technicians and CSR's can also review the person giving the script. This teaches them to look for the critical elements in the script and presentation.

This system is as professional as it gets. It rivals any sales system in use by any company. If you're serious about your company and you really understand the necessity to grow and systemize your business, and you want to get maximum sales and profits from your business… you need professional-grade tools to do it with.

You also get all of the presentations for carpet, tile, area rugs, and upholstery cleaning.

You get forms for measuring up the house that clearly shows the pricing for the three different packages, as well as a master chart that shows what is contained in each of the packages.

You also get daily and weekly report forms that will allow you to absolutely track the performance of each and every technician. The daily report contains all of the critical information for the daily performance of that technician.

8.

What The Sales System Will Do For You

This system is based around the idea that the technician and the CSR aren't just answering the phone and cleaning carpet, they are actually in a very powerful position to sell.

By giving them an easy to follow script that isn't cheesy or high-pressure, you can easily make sales that your company isn't even coming close to right now.

Most technicians don't want to do this, because they'd rather not... but truly... it's EASY to do! Anyone can do it. Even a reluctant technician... and all of a sudden that technician is making more money than they ever have!

This system allows you to use a very sophisticated and effective sales system in a very easy and non-threatening way.

The customers love the fact that they have a choice... They won't even notice that they are choosing a service level that is higher than they would have otherwise!

You'll know the numbers and the performance of every technician, so it can be easily managed. You'll know exactly what to do.

This is the same system I used to sell for $50,000 to the large companies and it can easily add between $50 and $100 to you average job size. That means on average, $50 to $100 MORE on every job you do! Over the course of a year that's easily tens of thousands of increased PROFIT... bottom line money that you get to keep!

> DISCLAIMER: There is no guarantee of performance or results with this system. Your actual performance could be more or less than this.

What this thing can really do for you is allow you to get yourself free, by paying for your way out of the traps we talked about earlier.

You can take this money and invest it in systems for your business, the support you'll need to follow-through, better equipment, more employees, profitable marketing, and predictably grow your business to a million-dollar, level three company.

When your CSR's and technicians are on the system, you'll know your customers are getting the full story on what makes your company unique, and worth the extra money you're charging. This is critical to building a high-end profitable company.

Your customers will also get a consistent story no matter who they talk to.

Your jobs will be easier, faster, and more profitable

It sells without the shell game, so it provides a better customer experience.

Because it increases the amount of money you get out of each customer, this system allows your marketing to work better. Campaigns that once were unprofitable, now can work!

9.
The Marketing System

Earlier, we talked about the three ways you can grow your business. Marketing, so that you have more customers, is probably the most obvious way you can do this.

In the last ten years, it seems nearly everyone has a marketing system out, some are decent, some are just re-hashes of what everyone else is saying, and a few are downright awful.

These packages are usually sold as the 'cure' for an ailing business, because they provide more money. Here is the truth about that however: Marketing alone won't fix a business.

In fact, many times throwing a ton of work at someone who is already having trouble managing it all will just make the problems worse.

There has to be a structure in place to hang all of that growth on or else the business will collapse under the weight of it all.

This doesn't always make sense, since most carpet cleaners' biggest problem, is that they aren't making enough money. You would think that if they could just get some more business, everything would be alright and all their problems would be solved.

As the saying goes, "If you're in a hole, you can't get out by digging faster!"

In this section I'll describe a proven system that works. This system is based on marketing systems that I've designed for the most successful companies in the industry.

This will get you more work, but as you'll see, this system makes sense. There really aren't 400 things you can do to get new business. Not 400 things that really work anyway. It's easy to think up of a bunch of ideas that might conceivably bring someone to the point of doing business with you, but it's very unprofitable to actually do all of those things.

What you need are a few strategies that work, and that work really well. You need to be able to track them so that you know that they are making you money instead of costing you a fortune.

A good marketing system will allow you to profitably grow your business. This gives you control over your growth. It gives you the ability to 'dial-in' exactly how many customers you need, and know exactly what you've got to do to get them, and how much it's going to cost.

With all the marketing systems out there, there really aren't any that I've seen that can truly do that.

You're about to learn exactly what works, how to look at marketing, and how to measure it in a way that will allow you to make money from it.

You'd think that's what everyone would do, but unfortunately most of them don't.

This is only a part of your business, however. Your marketing system works alongside the other two systems to give you control and freedom from your business.

Marketing Blunders

First, I'd like to talk about some things NOT to do. These marketing blunders are responsible for a lot of confusion about marketing.

A lot of it really gets back to being diligent about tracking and really understanding some key principles. A lot of people think that they know this stuff, and unfortunately they just don't.

In addition, there is a bit of an unknown quantity when it comes to marketing. You can run a very successful campaign that makes you tons of money at one time of the year… and then later on you run it again, and it flops.

For that reason, marketing has to be looked at in context with everything else. It relates to the other things going on around it.

You can make someone an offer for 15% off, during Spring and be covered up in work, (If you do it right!) but make that same offer during Winter when the snow is flying and it may fall flat on it's face!

These blunders are things people do whose marketing isn't working for them. Obviously these are things you should never do.

Don't understand return

If you look at many of the marketing programs out there in this industry, you'll see claims like, "I paid $1,000 and got $2,000 back in only a week… I doubled my money in a week! That's a 5000% yearly return on my money!!!!"

Well, not exactly. This person probably broke even. Understanding this is critical. If you think you're making money when you're really not, you're going to get into trouble... and pretty quick!

Failing to account for costs

This is related to the first one. People often make very big assumptions in this business, and some of them are way off base. It's been my experience that very few cleaners, even the big ones, really know what their costs are.

Failing to account for discounts

Ready for a simple test? Think about this: If you're making a 15% profit margin... and you run a campaign offering 20% off... How much money did you make?

This one is of course related to 'not accounting for costs'. If you don't know how much room you have, you may end up wondering, after all the marketing you've been doing, exactly where all the money went?

Examining marketing results in a vacuum

Marketing... especially the results of marketing, is closely related to many other things going on in your business. Marketing does not exist in a vacuum. It relates with other areas, and you have to know that, and know how it relates, or you won't know when things are working and when they're falling apart.

No overall marketing plan

Most carpet cleaners don't market at all. Of those that do, most don't have a clearly laid-out plan of when the various campaigns will be run, what the offers are, and what media they will use, etc.

This requires a lot of careful thought and planning in advance. Unfortunately, the cleaners that fail to do this, often end up buying advertising from whoever walks in their door selling it this week.

This just doesn't work well.

No targeting

Marketing to people who don't want, can't afford, or don't need your services is a complete waste of time and money... and yet carpet cleaners insist on doing it every day in every city in the country!

Simple targeting can make all the difference in whether a campaign is profitable or not.

No measurement

Very few people really measure the results of their advertising well enough. Most people, however, really mean to! They want to measure their results, but they are often unclear as to exactly how to do it... or they get really busy... or they aren't in the office when the phone rings, and so they can't write the results down in the proper place.

These are all really good reasons. But what happens is that when it's time to make important decisions about what advertising to invest in... these people have no clue. They feel out of control because they don't have the information to make the right decision.

You need a system to track every call, including the source and the job size. Ideally you'll need to know things like, has this customer bought before, and if so, when?

No effective message

Most advertising doesn't really contain a 'message'. Of those that do, most are weak and watered down.

The customer needs to hear certain things if they're going to buy, and if your ad doesn't tell them, they'll move right along to someone else who's doing a better job of telling their story.

This is doubly true if you're trying to charge them more than everyone else in your town! Your advertising needs to back you up!

Living off response instead of customer base

This may sound a little weird at first. What I'm really saying here is that you have a group of customers that do business with you...

This group calls you again and again, and if that group were to double in size, you'd have a company that was twice the size that it is now.

What most people do, is they market when they need the money. (That's assuming they can afford it!) When things are good, they are far too busy to market.

This is the kiss of death!

You'll never get ahead this way.

Living off response is what people do when they are worried about getting that next job, because they need the money... and they spend all of it!

If you live off your customer base, that means you know that on average, each customer calls you every 14 months, or every two years... whatever it is. You know what your average job size is. In other words, you know what each customer is worth to you.

You have clear, well-thought-out systems for getting new customers and for keeping the ones you have...

You might say that it's a long-term versus a short-term viewpoint.

Failing to nurture customers

This is one that gets almost everyone! Almost no one does a really good job at keeping in touch with, and retaining, their customers.

Customers aren't owned by any company. If they feel mistreated, they'll usually vote with their feet... and go somewhere else where they feel appreciated.

This may not be 'fair', but it is what it is, and failing to acknowledge this fact is dangerous at best!

Amazingly enough, there is always a ton of money in the current customer base... just waiting for the carpet cleaner to pick it up. But almost no one does... at least not nearly as well as they could!

It really makes no sense to go to all of the trouble of building a customer base, keeping track of them, paying huge money to various advertisers to get these customers to call—only to ignore them and let them slip away through in-attention, and yet this is so common, it's more the norm than the exception.

Understanding Marketing Concepts

When you talk about marketing in this industry, you get a lot of theory. Theories are fine, but if they don't work in the real world, they won't do you any good.

As you read through this section, you'll find that you aren't likely to find anyone else who looks at marketing quite like this.

Almost everyone makes marketing way too simplistic... and it's not that it's particularly complicated, but sometimes it is. Many times, when carpet cleaners try to implement a strategy, they find it doesn't work for them.

Marketing doesn't have to be difficult, and it really isn't. But there are a few areas that are hard to pin down. There is a science to it, but overall, it isn't an exact science, if that makes any sense.

What I'm saying is that marketing needs to be as practical and real-world as possible… and yet, there are still areas that defy logic. Things that don't seem to make sense.

Personally, I have been a direct-response advertising consultant, and as you know, I've worked with a lot of large carpet cleaners.

What I've found is that it's very difficult to fit everything into one box.

What I mean by that is that although direct-response advertising makes sense on many levels, it isn't the end-all, be-all that the people selling the direct-response packages would have you believe.

These are marketers remember…

So, rather than try to cram everything into a box labeled 'direct-response', I'd rather approach things from a standpoint of 'what works', and take it from there.

You'll find that many elements of direct-response are still here, and still apply.

But you'll also find other things that have allowed many people to build huge companies.

I'd be doing you a disservice if I didn't talk about these techniques as well.

Marketing Doesn't Stand Alone

You can't really look at marketing in a vacuum... It doesn't stand alone. It relates to everything around it, and everything else in the business.

For instance, let's say you want to figure out if a certain campaign has made you money or not. That can depend greatly on what your costs are.

I'm not talking about your costs to market, although that applies too... but that's obvious– I'm talking about the costs to actually do the work.

A campaign might work for one company, but be a miserable failure for another one, simply because the second company is less efficient at getting the work done.

Let's say you want to track the source of a call– The customer calls in and they looked you up on the internet... but they're also a previous customer– so which is it... previous customer or internet lead?

Your marketing is also closely related to your sales systems and abilities within your company.

If you have a strong sales system that clearly conveys what makes you unique and sells each customer a lot of your services, then your marketing will work well, because you'll have a bunch of return on your money.

If your sales system is weak, and your average job size is small, you may find that it's really hard to get any marketing to work well.

This is because your return on your investment is so low.

Marketing relates to, and interacts with, everything around it.

That is <u>A</u> truth… but it isn't necessarily <u>THE</u> truth!

What I mean by that is, you still have to look at marketing by itself to understand it.

Then you have to try and fit that understanding into the real world to decide what it means.

Two Critical, Absolute-Must, Goals For Your Marketing

For your marketing to be effective, it really only has to do two things:

1. First, it has to keep as many of your current customers as possible.
2. Second, it needs to profitably attract new customers.

These are two very different things, and so your marketing has to approach each goal differently.

This gives you growth. You can't ever have growth if you aren't keeping your customer base that you've already earned… and you can't afford growth if you can't grow profitably.

This is harder than it sounds, and it's harder to define than it sounds.

For instance, let's say you're running a small carpet cleaning company and you have no business at all, so you did a marketing campaign and brought in $10,000 a month in total revenue.

This is all just an illustration, so don't get hung up on the actual numbers here… I'm just trying to make a point.

So let's say that your 'hard' cost, which is your labor, your chemicals, your gas, wear and tear on your van, etc., is $4,000 for that month.

In addition, let's say your 'soft' cost, or overhead is another $4,000.

So, after the dust clears, you are making $2,000 in profit for that month.

So your profit margin is 20%.

Suppose you had to invest $2,000 in a campaign to produce that $10,000 worth of business.

When you subtract the money that you spent to get the $10,000 in business, you are left with nothing…

Total Revenue	$10000
'Hard' Cost	-$4000
'Soft' Cost	-$4000
Profit	=$2,000
Cost of Campaign	-($2,000)
(What's left over)	$0

Now you could look at this as an investment in the future, taking into consideration that these people will hopefully buy from you again in the future, but that's not profitable growth in the short-term.

It IS profitable in the long-term, PROVIDED that they actually do business with you in the future and pay you back for the investment you made.

Then you have to ask how long you can afford to wait to get your money back.

Now let's muddy the waters a little more.

Let's say you were ALREADY doing $10,000 a month in business, and you used the very same marketing campaign to produce an ADDITIONAL $10,000 in business.

So what I'm saying here is that you now brought in $20,000.

Your hard cost will now be $8,000.

But your overhead doesn't change… it's still $4,000.

Because your overhead is already paid, this campaign is now profitable for you.

Total Revenue	$20000
'Hard' Cost	-$8000
'Soft' Cost	-$4000
Profit	=$6,000
Cost of Campaign	-($2,000)
(What's left over)	$4000

The point here is that you ran the EXACT SAME CAMPAIGN, producing the EXACT SAME RESULTS, but because of where YOU were as a company, in one case it was profitable, and in another case it wasn't!

If your head is hurting right now, then you get the point I'm trying to make!

Many of the marketing gurus like to spout things like, "You can invest $1,000 and get $2,000 back… so that's doubling your money!"

And my point is that it depends greatly on your current situation.

These guys are over-simplifying because they want to sell products.

Doubling your money sounds great, who wouldn't want to do that? But again, the real-world is a little more complicated than that.

If you stick your head in the sand and blindly follow anybody, you're probably going to get into trouble.

So what you need in order to control your marketing is a framework that will allow you to look at your marketing in a way that you can calculate what it is really doing for you.

You also have to put that information in perspective with everything else that is going on in your business.

If you're running a successful, profitable company, it's a lot easier to find marketing strategies that will work and be profitable for you than if you're struggling and trying to make ends meet!

In practice, this example is ridiculous because in the first case, the person started out with no business at all!

What is more real-world is that the person might be in the middle somewhere, maybe he's bringing in $8,000 a month on his own and his hard costs are $3,000... his overhead is still $4,000, and he's making $1,000 a month after all the dust clears... then he launches this campaign.

What I'm trying to illustrate here, is how the results of a marketing campaign depend on everything else, and how determining what works isn't always as simple as it seems.

The Concept Of The Average Worth Of A Customer

Here is another principle which has great value. I will tell you right now, I'm going to over-simplify it in order to describe it.

What I'm talking about is the concept of the average worth, or average value of a customer.

Let's say you have 2,000 people in your customer list, these people each use you, on average, once every two years.

Simple math will tell us that this customer base will produce 1,000 carpet cleaning jobs each year.

If your average job size is $200, then this customer base will produce $200,000 in revenue each year for your company.

Now, let's say you want to become a one million dollar company...

How many customers are you going to need to support it?

Again, if your average job size is $200, you'll need a customer base of 10,000 customers in order to do that volume, and your company will have to produce 5,000 jobs each year, 416 jobs each month, 96 jobs each week, or 19 jobs each day… assuming a five-day workweek.

This is easy, simple, and it tells you a lot.

It isn't real, because we've completely taken away the possibility of commercial accounts, people that have cleaning done more frequently, etc… and yet, if we look at it as an average, it's surprisingly accurate!

Want to know how long it's going to take you to become a million-dollar company? This concept can tell you.

It will tell you how quick you have to grow to reach a certain goal, and if you plug in things like your attrition rate (how many customers you lose each year), it will tell you what's required to stay at your current level.

In this example, the average worth of a customer is $100 per year.

This is useful, because it supports the idea of keeping your customers. You will need a lot of customers in order to build a real business, and the whole basis of the business is the customer base.

You can grow from this place, but if you ignore them… which most carpet cleaners do… you simply can't market fast enough to keep up!

Each year, people move.

According to the US Census Bureau, anywhere from 16.0% to 17.3% of people moved in the US during the period of 1990 to 2000. Of those that moved, 56.2% stayed in the same county.

This means that each year, less than 10% of people move out of town.

(Almost no carpet cleaners measure their attrition rate. Even the big ones)

There are other reasons that carpet cleaners lose customers. Unfortunately, sometimes it's the carpet cleaner's fault!

Sometimes customers decide to use someone else. Sometimes a customer's brother-in-law will go into the carpet cleaning business.

From a practical standpoint, this tells us that:

1. It's probably a good idea to try to figure out what our attrition rate is.
2. We'd better count on losing around 15% of our customer base each year, whether we like it or not!

Obviously anything we can do to lower our attrition rate will help us out quite a bit.

Some of this attrition is preventable, and some of it isn't. Here's the problem: The only real way to measure attrition is to monitor how many people continue to use your services over a certain time period.

If you measure the time period over a short time, it won't be accurate. One year won't do it… You have to measure it over something like a three-year period for it to have any real meaning.

Unfortunately, this means that you won't really know if there's a problem until at least three years after the problem has already happened!

For this reason, then, you have to take a preventative approach to this whole thing.

You're far better off assuming there might be a problem, and trying to prevent it, then waiting until you know there's a problem and trying to fix it three or more years after the fact.

You prevent attrition by nurturing the relationship you have with your customers. I'm using that word 'nurture' intentionally.

It's a feminine word. It's like 'mothering', or protecting your customers. That's what it takes.

If you ignore them… they'll leave… and YOU'LL be left holding the bag–

And it will be an empty bag!

What happens is that carpet-cleaning business owners… get so focused on growth and on getting new customers, that they forget about or ignore the ones they already have.

This is probably just human nature at work. How many marriages are ruined by lack of attention and taking things for granted?

How many times does the grass seem greener somewhere else?

It's human nature to fail to appreciate what is right under our noses, and this is no exception.

The fact is, it's cheap to keep old customers coming back.

Let's say you mail something to them every two months, that's six contacts every year. Let's say you spend as much as $1 per contact, and again, that your customers do business with you every two years.

That means you are spending a whopping $12 over a two-year period to keep that customer! THAT'S ALL!

Many of the companies I've worked with have calculated that it takes as much as $96 to get a new customer!

Now I'm pretty sure you've heard this all before... most people have. But it's doing the basics well, that makes you successful.

Admittedly, I created a pretty sophisticated system of sales and management for this industry, and much of it is very new, at least for this industry.

That sophistication has power in it. But it's designed to work in addition to, not instead of, the basic things that are proven to work.

The best marketing system in the world isn't good enough to overcome not keeping your customers.

Just Because Someone Did Business With You Does NOT Mean They Are Your Customer!

Now THIS will challenge some people! (Which frankly, I kind of love doing...)

If you walk up to a carpet cleaner and ask them what the definition of a customer is, they'll usually respond with some version of, "Someone who I've done cleaning for."

You'd be amazed at how little this really means!

What I'm getting at is that most times, when a 'customer' calls a carpet cleaner, the carpet cleaner assumes they are now married to that customer... The carpet cleaner usually assumes that customer is now "Theirs!"

It's like the customer is now owned by the carpet cleaner... and it just isn't so.

In one study, after just three months, over 50% of customers couldn't remember the carpet cleaner they used... in most cases, THEY COULDN'T EVEN PICK THEM OUT OF THE YELLOW PAGES!

Think about that. Now these carpet cleaners were listed in the yellow pages... the point here is that the name of the company wasn't memorable to the customer at all.

The customer forgot who they used!

Because we're all busy, and this is just like most things... you either use it or lose it!

Once the customer's carpet had been cleaned, their problem went away... they no longer needed to think about carpet cleaning, and so they didn't!

Now it's probably not that they wouldn't remember you if you bumped into them on the street... but are they a loyal customer?

Business owners don't even like to think about this stuff. Most just deny it. They just say, "Not my customers... my customers all know and love me. They wouldn't dream of using anyone else!"

Really? Are you sure?

I have no doubt that you really want that to be true... but that alone doesn't make it true.

The reason I bring this up is that nearly everyone is absolutely horrible at keeping their customers!

A customer is someone that clearly understands what makes your company unique. Someone that really understands why you are the best choice for them. Someone that understands all of the advantages that you bring to the table.

And most people just don't care that much.

At least not unless you give them a reason to...

It's possible for someone to need for their carpets to be cleaned, and they call a company out of the phone book, and have it done and that is that!

The company gets paid, the customer is happy, because they got their problem solved... and the customer goes on about their busy life.

But there's no loyalty there.

If they needed cleaning again, the customer might call that company back... but then again, they might not.

They are under no obligation.

The point I'm making here, is that many carpet cleaners act as though they have succeeded when the customer calls...

In reality, they have an opportunity there, and it's great that the customer called... but it's only the first step in the relationship. The cleaner has to deepen the relationship and build loyalty or that customer is probably gone!

A 'captured' customer is an educated customer. They are probably referring you to others. They have an ability to talk about your services and they understand what makes you different, better, and unique.

In short, they... "get it". They get you...

They understand what you're about, and what you're trying to do with your business.

That's a customer! That's someone you can depend on. But it's up to you to make that happen. You can do that two ways:

First, you can manage the experience they have with you in the home. You can use the sales system to really explain to them why your company is superior.

Second, you can do it through marketing. You can regularly remind them why they should do business with you. You can make sure that they remain educated about the differences between carpet cleaners. You can make sure that they truly understand the advantages that your company offers them.

The Biggest Marketing Mistake You Could Ever Make

This all leads us to the biggest marketing mistake that a carpet cleaner can make: Living off response instead of living off the customer base.

The difference is a philosophical one.

A carpet cleaner that lives off of response is focused on getting the job.

A carpet cleaner that lives off the customer base is focused on getting the customer.

That's the difference, right there. But it's a huge difference.

In the one case, the carpet cleaner gets the job and basically throws the customer away. (Although they don't look at it that way... that's really what they do!)

The carpet cleaner that lives off of the customer base, is concerned with building an ongoing relationship with a group of people.

It's obvious which approach will work, isn't it?

You can spot which approach people are taking by looking at their marketing.

Your marketing needs to be filled with reasons why.

But most marketing is really focused on getting the job instead of getting the customer.

Obviously the bait and switch guys fall into the category of people who are just after the job, because after the experience their customers have... the customers will probably never call them back!

But what's interesting is that many direct-response-type ads are very job focused as well.

Now obviously you've got to get the job, because you get paid for those. But most marketing isn't based around the idea that you have to win the customer over to your way of thinking.

People often want to keep the ads short and not tell their whole story.

Or they resort to general phrases like, "We're the best!", or, "The leading carpet cleaning company!"

These phrases are completely meaningless because absolutely everyone says them. There is nothing behind them. They are empty, vacant, and worthless.

Don't use them. Instead, use words that really set you apart. Build the relationship between you and your customers.

This does mean something else that's interesting, however.

There are some customers that are simply not worth the trouble. You definitely know the ones I'm talking about!

If your business is built on relationships. I'm going to say that those relationships need to be win-win relationships.

In other words, you need to do business with people that don't waste your time and your energy.

If someone is too much trouble, get rid of them. You are under absolutely no obligation to do work for anyone. Who you choose to accept as a client is entirely up to you... You definitely have that right!

Occasionally you should exercise it!

The only thing that will help you grow your business is having a large group of dedicated, loyal, customers that sing your praises every chance they get.

So if you've got someone that complains and is never happy, and it gets to the point that they are more trouble to you than they are worth... cut them loose!

Again, if you're job-focused... you'll never do that, and sometimes you should!

How To Profitably Grow Your Business

If you've been around the industry for any length of time and kept your eyes open at all, you've no doubt heard of direct-response advertising.

You're also aware of the fact that there are two distinct camps when it comes to marketing a carpet cleaning business.

First, there are the traditional advertisers. This is often referred to as image advertising or institutional advertising.

Second, there is direct-response.

Image advertisers talk about building a brand and top-of-the-mind awareness.

Direct-response advertisers talk about rates of return and conversion. Because they are usually able to determine why a given customer calls, they are able to determine things like cost per lead, and cost per sale.

It seems that people are squarely in one camp or the other. It also seems that direct-response people don't want to have any thing to do with advertising that isn't direct-response... and institutional advertisers want to build brands and create awareness, and would rather not have anything to do with anything that resembles direct-response.

What I'm saying here is that these two seem to be opposing viewpoints, and there is very little tolerance for the other point of view.

I use to be a direct-response copy writer and consultant. I used to write direct-response pieces. I helped businesses develop campaigns. I love direct-response advertising, it's very powerful.

And yet...

If you look at the largest and most successful carpet cleaning companies in existence, you'll find that almost all of them used at least some image advertising and built a brand in their market.

This isn't a fluke, because you don't see it just in some places. It's everywhere.

What I'm trying to say here is that direct-response works... it's powerful alright, but it isn't everything.

You can't say that image advertising doesn't work, because it does... it just costs a fortune to do, that's all!

That's the downside of creating a brand... it's expensive.

That's why the marketing program that I recommend is composed of mostly direct-response-type ads, with some cheaper image-building strategies included as well.

This gives you a balanced mix.

Because it's nice to have a brand. And all of the really large companies do.

I'm going to assume that you don't have a lot of money to throw at marketing, and honestly I believe in the concept of being able to track things enough to lean toward the direct-response side of things pretty heavily.

If you want to dominate your market, and I'm assuming you do, you'll need to consider how to do that. It's possible to use direct-response-type marketing to dominate a market, at least the areas in your town that you want to dominate.

If you don't have top-of-the-mind-awareness in the trailer parks and apartment buildings in your town, that's okay... These people probably aren't prime candidates for your services anyway.

But it's possible to use the ability to target direct-response advertising so that you can build a brand within certain areas that contain large numbers of people that are likely to be your customers.

This makes sense, especially if you're just starting out, and you don't have a huge budget to advertise with.

I'm not aware of a huge company, that dominates their market that doesn't use at least some image advertising.

But let's talk about what that looks like.

These companies have advertising budgets. What they do is invest a certain percentage of their revenue back into marketing. So if they make $1,000, they might re-invest 10% back into marketing, or $100.

This way, they always have plenty of money to market with. As the company grows, so does the advertising budget.

Some of these companies get to where they are spending anywhere from $30,000 to $50,000 a month on marketing.

Now think about what happens when you invest that kind of money, and then use the power of targeted marketing!

This is a powerful concept, and you should definitely use it. This is one of the concepts that will allow you to continually grow.

When you're starting out however, you're a long way from this.

Investing In Marketing

Before we go any further, I'd like to talk about one of the 'rookie' mistakes made by many small carpet cleaners. This mistake will keep you small and will prevent you from being able to go very far with your business.

Your business needs marketing. You've got to promote it or it won't grow, it's as simple as that.

What often happens is that small carpet cleaners get it into their heads that they will invest in marketing 'later'... when they have enough money.

It just doesn't work like that!

What these owners are really saying is that they don't have any money right now, so they are going to wait until they do before they spend any money... to make any money!

Can you see the fallacy in that?

In most cases, these owners are taking the money that the business needs to support itself, the very life-blood of the business, and spending it on their own personal lives.

They can't market... but they have a big-screen TV.

They can't market... but they can go out to dinner.

If you rape and pillage your business, there is no way it can produce for you.

If you put that money back into the business, then it can grow strong, and in time, it will be able to provide you with every creature comfort you can imagine.

But there isn't a free lunch... if you don't invest now... you won't have the return later.

This is how carpet cleaners go under.

You might have to take drastic measures to cut expenses in your life, if you've let yourself get over-extended, but you've got to invest in your business, or it can't and won't grow.

You can't wait until some future time when things are grand and you have 'extra money' lying around to invest in the very thing that will feed and support you. Do it now.

Being Offer-Driven

One of the big decisions you have to make when you start out, or even later on... is whether to become an offer-driven company or not.

Like most things, there are positives and negatives to this approach.

Despite what you've heard about it, I'd like to have a common-sense discussion with you about this. Just see if any of this makes sense to you:

The Upsides:

Making an offer along with your advertising is the thing that allows you to track how well it's working. When someone responds, wanting a certain offer that you've promoted in a certain media... you know how they heard about you, so you know your advertising worked... AND you know how well it worked based on the number of responses you got.

The offer also greatly increases response. You're basically giving people an enticement to call now. There is something in it for them if they pick up the phone... so they do!

Rather than waiting, they act now so they can get some bonus or reward.

In general, the stronger the offer, the better the response.

The Downsides:

One of the biggest problems with becoming an offer-driven company is that over time, the customers learn that your prices aren't real.

In extreme cases of this, companies send out direct-response pieces to their customer base every month, or sometimes even more frequently than that. And every piece they send has some sort of offer on it.

It doesn't take a scientist to figure out that if a company is always offering 20% off their prices, then their prices aren't real. It's a very small jump in the customer's mind to start thinking that they really don't have to 'CALL NOW', because the same sale, or one just as good, will be available next month!

This will shoot your response down completely. Once people realize what you're up to... that you're going to constantly market to them and you'll always be making offers, they really have no need to respond when you send them something… They can just call when they want and they'll always get an offer.

This completely negates any advantage of making the offer in the first place, because it teaches your customers that your prices aren't real.

Unfortunately, in many cases, the carpet cleaner hasn't really considered the cost of making the offers to their customer base.

What I mean is that not only do you have the cost of marketing, which can be considerable… but the carpet cleaner often seems to be so excited to get the work at all, that he completely forgets that all the work is coming in at 10, 15, or 20% less than it normally would!

The profit margins in this business are not that high. So in order to make an offer like that, you pretty much have to raise your prices by 20%, so that you can then give your customer 20% off, and still come out okay.

This becomes something of a shell game… and if your customers ever realize you're playing a game with them, they are going to resent it.

I know of many companies that brag about how high their prices are, but it's been years since they've actually done a job at those prices… if ever!

Discounting

When you say the word 'discounting', it often brings up images of the typical $9.95 per room carpet cleaners.

These carpet cleaners are the kings of discounters. But if you examine the idea of discounting, you'll find that it really means that your getting something of value for a lot less than it's really worth.

There are discount superstores, there are discount catalogs, there are discount chains...

They are all based around the idea that you can go in there and get a deal of some kind. They are based on the idea that you can take advantage of a situation and make it work to your benefit.

We all love to feel like we saved money and got an incredible deal... especially if we got a better deal than anyone else could have.

The problem with discounting is that it usually doesn't work out all that well for the seller. Now if you happen to be a major national or international chain, and you are able to buy at a ridiculously cheap level because of your volume, and because you have teams of people that negotiate very hard, that's one thing.

But how does that relate to you being a fairly small carpet cleaner? Even the giants of the industry are too small to discount. They may have some economy of scale, but it's not that big.

The other problem is the basis of the transaction. What I mean is that if the whole transaction is done based on the idea that the customer has to somehow get this larger-than-life steal-of-a-deal... yes, you might get the job, but are you sure you want it?

There won't be any loyalty there... How could there be? The basis of your transaction is that you allowed someone to take advantage of the situation.

Now in our culture, this is done all the time, and I don't think that people think it through very much.

I love a deal as much as the next person... but I don't want to put anyone out of business when I do it! I'm willing to pay a fair price as long as I get good service and good quality.

I know I'm not going to get something for nothing. There isn't any free lunch. But the idea of a 'free lunch' is promoted almost continuously! It's all around.

Unfortunately some carpet cleaners have decided that this must be the path to growing their businesses, and they've tried to do this.

I've seen a rather disturbing trend lately. I've started to see coupons in my mailbox advertising carpet cleaning for $8.95 a room!

Think about that! It's a dollar cheaper!! What is scary is that it probably works. So now some carpet cleaner has figured out a way to attract customers based on the idea that $9.95 for a room of cleaning is just too damned expensive!

No doubt someone else will start marketing the idea of $7.95 per room... Where does it stop?

The idea behind all of this is that if you can just get the customer to call... even if it is a ridiculous offer, then somehow maybe you can turn the whole thing around... Somehow you'll be able to make it work for you.

Even if it doesn't work for you on this job, maybe you'll be able to make it all back on future business somehow.

At least you got the job... right?

I'm sure you see the problem. What happens when some other cleaner makes an even better offer than the one you did?

Now I know the theory here just as well as you do, but does it work?

The theory is that you go into this customer's house and you do such an incredible job... providing such an incredibly high level of service that they acknowledge that you are the absolute best service provider that they have ever seen in their entire lives... and now they've seen the light.

From now on, they no longer want a deal.

No sir, not for them. Their lives are changed.

It's the straight and narrow from now on for them. From now on, they'll pay top-dollar for your services no matter what other offers anyone makes them.

Even if you completely stink at follow-up... and make no effort to keep in touch with them... that carpet cleaning they got was a show-stopper, so they're your customer from now on!

Is it just me, or do you see a problem with this theory?

Now, obviously I'm being rather flippant here, but this really is the business model that many... maybe even most, carpet cleaners are trying to use.

When it comes to discounting, there are two problems:

First, most cleaners can't really afford to do it. The simple truth is, most cleaners have absolutely no idea what it costs them to do a job. They are so happy to get the job at all... that they don't ask questions, they just do the job and cash the check.

Second, the whole basis of the transaction is wrong if you discount. If you make someone an unbelievable offer in order to get their business, you are in effect, training them as to what to expect next time. You really can't blame them if they want the same thing the next time they call... wouldn't you?

And then of course on the other side, discounting works. It makes the phone ring. It gets people to respond.

Doing direct-response without making an offer, breaks every rule there is about how to use direct-response!

So what do we do?

First of all, let's look at when we are able to discount. We can make less on a job in order to get a customer... but we can't make nothing.

If you're making a 15% profit margin... you can't give a 20% discount. If you do that a lot, you'll have the experience of being busy, and not having any money, which is a bad combination!

If your soft costs are paid, then you have some more room, so you COULD make the argument that you are able to give a steeper discount and still make money.

You have to consider the effect on your customers though.

If you make your customers an offer every month, very quickly they're going to realize that you ALWAYS have a sale and that they can pretty much call whenever they want and still get a 'deal'.

Of course they are also going to realize that your 'deals' aren't really deals at all. They represent what you are willing to do business for. In other words, these are your real prices.

In practice, it's okay to give a discount once in a while, but your customers can't get the impression that it's something you do all the time.

If you do give your customers a discount, they've got to realize that there is a reason for it, and they shouldn't get the impression that they can always get that discount.

There is another hidden cost to discounting. Many times, carpet cleaners will discount in order to get new customers to call. Many times, current customers will call and ask for the same discount.

You could also argue that it's possible that some current customers that would have used you anyway, will respond to an offer and therefore you are giving them a discount that you really didn't have to give them... There really is no way to measure this, and you can't really do anything about it, so it's probably best not to worry too much about it. I do think that it's important to realize that this happens, however, and that there is some cost associated with it.

I have seen companies slowly destroy their ability to market by making repeated, frequent offers to customers. (Like sending them an offer every month) This doesn't happen all at once, but it happens over time. It probably takes about two years to really set in, but once it does, it's very hard to undo.

The lifetime value of a client is real. A customer is valuable over time, because they can use your services again and again.

For this reason, it's worth it to spend money to get a new customer. An introductory offer is fine, but you have to clearly explain why you're making them this offer and why you won't be able to do it again!

This makes the offer real.

It's fine to do occasional yearly offers or anniversary offers.

Making offers is like adding salt to something you're cooking. If you add the right amount, it's delicious and it brings out the flavor. If you add too much, it completely ruins it!

So what I recommend is that you become a partially offer-driven company. You will make offers, but you will do them sparingly. You won't have a sale running all the time.

Of course if you're going to ever make an offer, you have to be able to make a profit doing it. For that reason, you have to raise your prices so you have the room to offer a discount and still be able to make something on the job.

You can do consistent marketing all the time, however. This marketing will focus on telling your story. You need to clearly convey what makes you unique and better. That's the purpose of your marketing. Remember the concept of going after the customer instead of going after the job.

You want to educate your customers so that they really understand what you're all about… so they 'get' you, and realize the value you bring to the table. They have to understand that you're not just another carpet cleaner, but that you're someone who understands their needs, and what they're looking for when they have someone come into their home to do a service for them.

Tracking Your Marketing

Most carpet cleaners market because they know they should. But they don't keep track of what works and what doesn't. It's not always the easiest thing to do. So they market and they determine what works based on if they're busy or not.

This seat-of-the-pants approach wastes huge amounts of money and makes it impossible to ever really know why your company is growing... or not.

Tracking your marketing isn't that hard. All you need is a system... a method, for doing it.

All this means is that you have to know your costs for each campaign. You'll only be able to track campaigns that have some type of an offer unless they are referral campaigns.

The very best way to keep track of the results of your advertising is to have the person answering the phones get the source of the call.

This won't happen unless you have a script that gets used on every call, as well as a call log that the CSR (Customer Service Representative) fills out for every call.

You need to do some management of that position in order to make sure that everything is happening as it should, and part of this management is that you'll probably need to invest in a system to record the calls coming into your office.

A system like this can be bought for as little as $200 to $300, and it will be very valuable in monitoring the CSR's... not just for capturing the source of your calls, but also to monitor how effectively they are selling.

At the end of the campaign or at the end of the month, you can take all the information from the call logs and enter it onto a report form that will allow you to calculate the return on investment, conversion rate, average cost per job, and many other useful items.

Then, when you have to make a decision regarding what type of advertising to use, you'll have the information as to what works and what didn't. After you do this, all your advertising decisions become obvious. Without this, the advertising decisions will remain a mystery.

Making The Most Of Your Advertising Dollars

The very worst thing you could possibly do, is to spend all the time, effort, and money it takes to get 100 new customers, and then forget or disappoint them.

How many times have you seen a movie where the studio spent tens of millions of dollars promoting it… they spent tens of millions more, hiring the biggest stars… they spent tens of millions more, getting the best directors… and finally, $100 million dollars later, the movie tanks.

Why?

Because it wasn't a good movie, that's why!

You just can't market fast enough or well enough, to overcome lousy quality or bad experiences.

On the other hand, I'm sure you've seen some obscure movie that didn't have a marketing budget at all, there were no big names in it, the director was unknown…but before you know it, everyone's talking about it, simply because it was a really good movie.

I bring this up because many times people get the order wrong.

First, you have to have quality. You need quality at a level so that you really stand out... The kind of quality where people are referring you without you even asking them to. (And I don't mean your brother-in-law...) You need to be extraordinary.

Then, when you market, you can blow the roof off the thing! Then, you've really got something to sell! At that point... you're almost unstoppable.

But sometimes people get it backwards. They want to worry about quality later. People are often focused on marketing because they need the money, and the quality is allowed to slip.

I know of several carpet cleaning companies where quality is bad and marketing dollars don't seem to work anymore.

People don't respond because they know the company doesn't do a good job.

None of this stands alone. It is all inter-connected.

In theory, it's possible to do a really first-rate job with run-down, dirty equipment... but I can tell you it never happens.

There is the principle of 'how you do something, is how you do everything'.

If the equipment is run-down and dirty, I can absolutely guarantee that the quality will be lacking. This will always be true because the equipment is a reflection of the quality. If it was a top-quality company, the equipment would never be run-down and dirty!

You see this same principle when it comes to management. Management is an area where you probably need systems and procedures more than any other place. And yet many carpet cleaners stubbornly refuse to use something that would make them better, because they think that what they have is 'good enough'.

You want to know a huge truth about management?

Here it is:

"The quality of the company is equal to the quality of the management."

There is another thing that I've seen companies do as they grow, that really doesn't make any sense.

This one probably won't affect you until you become a larger level two or a level three company.

What I'm talking about is the tendency to quit doing what's working. Sometimes owners of businesses will talk themselves into or out of something just because they're bored with it.

A classic example of this is newsletters.

A newsletter is one of the proven things in this business. It absolutely works! No question about it.

Many small companies have built themselves up by using newsletters. But then something interesting happens...

At some point, they get to where they have 20,000 customers in their database.

Now this is what they've been trying to do all along. And they finally got there. For years now they've been religiously keeping in touch with their customers. And their customers keep coming back.

Everyone is happy.

Until one day when the owner looks at the cost of mailing a newsletter to 20,000 people!

"There must be a cheaper way..." he tells himself.

So what do you suppose happens?

That's right...

You guessed it.

He starts sending out postcards to save money!

Now a postcard is useful for some things. It's great if you're trying to make someone a short, specific, offer.

But it's a lousy way to tell your story. There just isn't enough room!

So, all of a sudden, the customer base is getting offers instead of a story.

Well, they're already getting offers from just about everyone... so what makes you unique now?

That's right... nothing!

And what happens is the percentage of returning customers drops like it fell off a cliff.

But hey... at least the owner's saving money, right?

He's gonna need to!

Marketing Strategies

Let's get into the actual strategies you'll use to grow your business.

These are the strategies that have been proven to work. I'm not saying that there aren't others out there than may also work, but these are proven and I know they work.

They've been successfully used by my clients all over North America.

These are the strategies that the 'big boys' of the industry pay me the money for. I didn't invent them, but I've made a careful study of what works and what doesn't.

I've also carefully 'tweaked' these strategies so that they work better.

As you might imagine, doing what I do, I've seen an awful lot of strategies. I've seen a lot of dismal failures... but I've also seen some remarkable successes.

You don't need 50 or 100 strategies to grow your business. What you need are a few that work!

The 'super-giants' of the industry didn't build up their companies by doing 50 different things.

There are a lot of marketing ideas out there, but most of them are just that... ideas.

What often happens is that the carpet cleaner tries a few of them, and they don't work very well, and the carpet cleaner gives up.

Back to the drawing board.

It's important to realize that you can't just go out and 'do' some direct mail, because that won't work... you've got to do direct-mail right.

What that means is that you either have to learn how to write your own copy, or buy your copy from a proven source. Unfortunately, it's harder than you might think to find someone that really understands direct-response advertising.

That's why in this system, I include all of the marketing pieces pre-built. All you have to do is plug in your company name, phone number, and a few things like that... and you're ready to go.

The other really great advantage is that all of the systems are completely, seamlessly, integrated... so they work with each other, and they all work to make YOU money!

But again, you have to track the money... you have to know your expenses... even with my stuff, you have to look at the whole picture or it won't work that well for you.

I'll tell you more about how to buy the system for your company later... right now, let me describe the strategies that are proven to work:

Current Clients

This area is an absolute must. Doing this is really simple and easy. It's not hard at all... it just takes a decision to do it. In other words, you have to be willing to spend the money.

Neglecting this area is what almost everyone does, but if you aren't going to keep your customers, it kind of makes everything else you're doing a little pointless doesn't it?

The Newsletter–

By far, this is the most effective way to keep in touch with your customers. As far as marketing campaigns go, it's also one of the most expensive.

A few points about this:

First of all, you've got to send an actual newsletter, with several different items of interest. It should be laid out like a little magazine with short, catchy, articles that pull the reader in. You will be mailing to a diverse group of people, so there ideally should be something for everyone in there.

The thing that makes a newsletter worthwhile in spite of the cost is the fact that it is so targeted. I mean, think about it… this is a mailing that is going out to your customers. You couldn't possibly come up with a better list than that!

A newsletter needs to have a feature article and it should be something that is relevant to the customer, interesting to them, and also something that makes you look good.

I've said it before, but you just can't accomplish this with a postcard, there's not enough room.

So what does the financial reality of a newsletter look like? Let's say you send a newsletter out six times a year (which is a minimum) and you have a customer list that has 2,000 customers in it.

You can have 2000 full color newsletters printed for under $1,100.

This isn't some cheesy newsletter though. It's an 11 X 17, printed in full-color gloss (like a magazine). It's folded into a brochure and then tri-folded for mailing.

You can have it mailed first-class, AND printed for $1,772.75. (These prices are as of this writing, and they might change, but probably not by much)

So that's a total of 0.89¢ a piece per customer.

Now, if you do this six times a year, you'll spend a total of 0.89¢ X 6 = $5.34 each year, mailing to each customer.

Let's add a dollar to that so you can send them a yearly reminder mailing, and you have a grand total of $6.34 per customer, per year.

Now let's say that on average, your customers use your services every two years. What that means is that over a two-year period, it will cost you $12.68 to maintain your relationship with that customer.

But what a relationship you'll have!

They'll pretty much think you're the only carpet cleaner in town!

Now of course they'll still get the other offers in their mailbox, everyone does. But you're making a point to educate them, and so they have the right information so they can understand what those other offers really mean (bait and switch, etc.) and they won't fall for them.

Now, typically it costs between $50 and $100 dollars (and sometimes more than that) to attract a new customer...

Or, you could keep the ones you've already got for $12.68. Are you convinced yet?!!

Do you see why this makes such sense? Why you've just GOT to do it?

Email–

You can also keep in touch with your customers by email, but you'll need a program to do it. Now that's not such a big deal, there are many that will. But again, you've got to do this right in order to be effective.

I know one friend of mine that is just larger-than-life. Everyone loves him. He's got an email list you'd have to see to believe. But he's got a problem...

You see, everyday, he thinks of something that his entire list really needs to know, so he sends them an email telling them about it.

Sometimes it's two emails a day! ... Or THREE!

What happened is people started requesting to be taken off his list. It was just too much!

So the point is, if you're going to send emails, send them sparingly, because people have very little tolerance if they feel like you're bugging them.

Obviously emails are much faster, cheaper, easier to send... and many other things than a newsletter. Some companies have tried to rely on email solely as a way to keep in touch with their customers.

This doesn't work nearly as well.

Now I have some ideas as to why this is, but they are only opinions. I think that spam is so prevalent that it's harder to get an email read.

I think that the fact that you're reading something in the virtual world, doesn't seem to have the impact that something physical does for most people.

People often have more than one email address, and they may give you one that is designed to catch their 'junk'.

You're the one that wants the relationship initially, not usually them. They may in time, understand how valuable that is, but at first, you can't blame them for trying to filter out unnecessary information from their life.

I think the email campaign has it's place, and the companies with the highest customer retention do both newsletters and email

Referral—

Now admittedly this is a strategy for getting new clients, not for getting your current clients to repeat. I include it here because you have to market to your current clients in order to get them to refer anyone.

The referral system is very simple. It can represent a steady stream of new clients for your business.

Referral sources are paid 10% of the job total for referring work to your company. So if someone refers a person that has $350 worth of carpet cleaning done, the person that referred them would get $35. That is issued as a credit, they can have the cash, or they can have cleaning done.

The best way to do this is to issue them some type of credit voucher... basically a coupon that shows they have a credit and then they can either redeem the voucher for cash or they can use it for cleaning services at a later time.

You might wonder why you don't just send them a check? Quite a few of these vouchers will never be redeemed for anything! People will just forget about them or for whatever reason decide not to use them.

You have to be careful of a couple of things here. First of all, you have to be aware that you are issuing vouchers that are redeemable for cash.

So in a worst-case scenario, someone could refer you $20,000 worth of work. (What a great problem to have, huh?) The point I'm trying to make is that person could show up with his voucher and want you to write them a check for $2,000.

Now, again, this is a great problem to have, but it does mean that you have to have something set aside. Some companies report that only about ½ of the vouchers they issue are ever redeemed.

Second, you need to have some way of keeping track of this. It's pretty common that someone will lose their voucher but will still want their referral fee, either in cash, or in cleaning credit.

This is only fair, after all, they did help you grow your business right? So all I'm saying is that you need a contact manager program, or a file system that will tell you where you stand with all these potential referral sources, so that if they ever lose their certificates, you've still got an accurate record of what you owe them.

The potential power of this is huge! In theory, you've now got your entire customer base working for you, helping you to grow your business. In practice, it's a little less than that.

What people will do, is if they have an opportunity to refer you, they will. Owners of carpet cleaning companies often are unrealistic about the effects of starting a referral program... It's almost as if they expect their customers to get on the phone and cold-canvass all their friends!

This won't happen. What will happen is that if someone has a conversation about carpet cleaning, or inquires about it, they will pass along your name to their friend.

It's important that you get the source of the call, and your phone personnel have to really dig sometimes to get this.

Assuming your customer is an up-scale lady, she's probably not always going to remind her friends, "Be sure and tell them I referred you so that I can get my referral!"

And yet she will appreciate her referral, even if she didn't ask for it.

The point is, it's up to you to keep track of this.

Once you've paid someone a referral fee, do you think they are going to be pretty excited about referring you again?

Definitely.

What I would recommend is that you pay the person a referral on everything the referred customer does for a year. After that, they're yours.

A couple of other points:

First, don't try to wiggle out of the referral. You should be eager to pay them. People who refer a lot, often start by referring one. If they hear that the people they referred had a good experience and they end up getting paid... they'll probably give you many more.

So pay them already! Don't try to get out of it... In fact, you should be glad to pay for a referral. It's one of the best investments in your business you could make.

Second, you need to be sure that you have room in your prices for all of this. What I mean is you are going to give 10% to the person referring you.

You also may give a discount to the person that is trying you out for the first time. In this case, you are going to be discounting, in effect, for two different people. So you're going to have to be sure your prices give you the room to do this.

Strategies For New Clients

Alright, so this is the area where all of the growth comes from. You are going to need a lot of new clients if you're currently a level one company and you're trying to grow to a level three.

In addition, there is attrition...

People move, people change, and so you won't get 100% of your current customers back… You're going to get some percentage of them, but you'll need new clients to replace the ones that leave.

Direct Response Inserts–

This is an 8½ by 11 flyer that can be inserted in newspapers, magazines, bulletins, newsletters… basically anything that is going out to your target market.

It has been very effective because you can have them printed up very inexpensively and then you mass distribute them.

The flyer is divided into columns and it tells your whole story… how you make beer!

The story is continued on the back and at there is an offer that expires within a fairly short period of time.

This can be a very profitable piece, depending on where you place it.

Some of my clients in small towns have gone ahead and had it inserted into the newspaper, and that has worked very well.

If you live in a city of any size, you may decide that the newspaper just isn't cost-effective. In that case you could have it inserted into a local arts publication or something that targets the market you're after.

Website/Internet–

There are three ways that a website and the internet can be very profitable and provide a steady stream of new clients for your business:

- Pay-per-click advertising
- Search engine optimization
- Local search

Pay-per-click advertising (PPC) has pretty much replaced the yellow pages as the prime way that people search for carpet cleaning.

Most of your clients, if you're an up-scale carpet cleaner, (and I'm assuming you either are, or want to be) are busy professionals. They often spend their days at a computer. They check email several times a day, and if they need cleaning services, most of them will go to the internet to find a carpet cleaner.

Pay-per-click advertising lets you 'buy your way in' to the top of the search results. If the potential customer clicks on your ad, they are taken to your website and you are charged for the click.

Naturally you've got to have a website that does an incredible sales job, because all they have to do is hit the 'back' button, and they'll be taken back to all the other search results and the other pay-per-click advertisers.

As I write this book, in March of 2008, there are several different carpet cleaners doing pay-per-click advertising, but the competition is no where near as intense as it is in the yellow pages.

Because of this, the bid prices for each click are fairly low, and so it's possible to get a lead that calls in for a carpet job for about $15.

Assuming you close half of those leads, which is a little low, you end up with a cost per sale of $30 or less.

This makes this medium a great place to buy new customers, because it's cheap... about 1/3 the cost of getting a customer from the yellow pages.

As time goes on, and more and more companies realize this and switch to the internet, the costs will go up... which means that right now is a great time to use this strategy.

It is possible to do this yourself, but a really good firm can provide recordings of your calls and give you very precise information as to how well your Pay-per-click campaigns are working.

The other way to use a website is Search engine optimization. This is where you carefully design and modify keywords and phrases on your site in order to get your site to come up on it's own, at the top, or near the top of the search results.

This takes more time, but the results are worth it. You generally need someone who knows how to do this for you in order to optimize your site, but it can be well worth the investment.

Most of the large companies are getting a lot of work from the internet, and there is no reason you can't do the same.

One of the huge benefits of the PPC campaign is that you can choose how much money you are willing to invest each day, week, and month, and the system will automatically rotate you into top position until your money is spent.

The system will also figure out your cost per click and position you so that you are getting the maximum bang for your buck, which interestingly may mean that you're not in the top position.

You can buy as many clicks as you want, and start and stop whenever you choose.

Because of this tremendous flexibility, and because of the truly massive numbers of people searching for carpet cleaning on the internet, this is a key strategy for growing your business.

Local Search is basically the map that you see that comes up on Google when you do a search for something.

This map happens to be positioned squarely in the middle of the most-looked-at part of the page, and so getting yourself top position in that list is critical.

Obviously if you do all three of these strategies, when someone searches for 'carpet cleaning'... it's going to look like you own the web!

Yellow pages–

Yellow pages used to be the mainstay of how you promoted a carpet cleaning company. What has happened in recent times is that the costs of yellow pages advertising has gone through the roof, and the response and results have died off. This combination is largely due to the internet and people searching there instead of the yellow pages.

The system that I sell includes yellow pages ads for carpets. This is because in some parts of the country, the population may not be as technically savvy as they are in the cities.

For instance, if you are located in a small town in Wyoming or Montana, you are still maybe going to want to do some internet advertising, and it won't cost you much to do… However, you'd probably still want to be listed in the yellow pages under carpet cleaning.

So when should you stay in the yellow pages and when should you get out? It's a very good question, and the answer will be evident when your yellow pages ad becomes unprofitable to continue.

Of course you won't know this without tracking your numbers religiously.

I can tell you that in most larger cities and towns, yellow pages advertising goes through times of the year when it is completely unprofitable… it's just too expensive to do… and it seems to be getting worse.

Most companies choose to have an in-column listing and heavily use the internet.

However, many companies still are able to show a decent rate of return using a smaller ad, like a quarter or half-page ad.

Having a yellow pages ad under rug cleaning still seems to work for most. This is probably because of the relative lack of competition in that category, and also because to dominate that category, you usually do not have to purchase a huge ad.

What I've described here is a trend, but as far as what you should do… you need to set up your system of tracking and find out for yourself. If you aren't currently in the yellow pages, and you are located in a fairly large city or town, I'd recommend that you consider the yellow pages as a way to promote your rug cleaning business, but I wouldn't recommend a heavy investment into a large yellow pages ad... you'll get further using the same dollars in other areas.

In most markets, there are also at least two competing yellow pages books. Many times, the secondary book is much cheaper than the primary book, and several cleaners have reported success advertising there, simply because the cost is small enough that it justifies the return.

Street mailing program–

This is a powerful strategy that will help you to dominate those areas in your town where your ideal clients live.

Let's say you do a job for Ms. Jones at 1234 Anyplace Ave. You can do a search on the internet, and pull all of the names and addresses of the people that live on her street.

Then, you'll send out a letter explaining that you've just done work for Ms. Jones at 1234 Anyplace Ave., and give them your story and make them an offer. This is similar in principle to the 'five-around' strategy with door hangers, except that you're mailing to the whole street.

This strategy basically is a cold mailing to people who don't know you. It works much better than a typical cold mailing would, however. This is because people identify with the real person that you identify as your client in the letter. They may not know them, but this person lives just down the street from them, so they feel a kinship with them. They connect with them.

It's not impossible for the person that is considering using your services to stop by and ask this person about their experience with you.

This feeling of connectedness makes your services not such an unknown quantity and increases response.

In addition to mailing the street that the initial customer lives on, you could also mail additional streets in the same area, but the further away you get from the initial customer, generally speaking, the less effective the response rate. In practice, it drops off rather sharply when you leave the customer's immediate area.

This strategy can be used effectively to farm an area. If you have an area where you do a lot of work, and it's not too big... say it's an area with 200 homes in it, every time you do a job in that area, you can let the whole neighborhood know about it. After about six months or a year of this, people that live in that area, will have the impression that quite literally all of their neighbors use you to clean their carpet, and of course they probably will too.

Visibility–

This is a powerful strategy that has been successfully used by some of the really big companies across the USA. Basically, you want to be visible. Meaning you want to have a location preferably on a busy street and you want to have your vans everywhere.

Some people have gone so far as to buy old decrepit vans that don't run, and they'll have them freshly painted and wrapped and they will park them at strategic locations around town.

These basically act as cheap billboards.

In practice, it's hard to track, or know how much this strategy is worth, but what visibility does, is it adds to the other campaigns you are doing.

It is a proven fact that when you run two campaigns within the same market, the response off the two campaigns is greater than the sum of the two campaigns run individually. Each campaign supports the other one.

Visibility helps you to build a name and a brand. That is something that you want to do, but I would recommend doing it through the use of the other techniques outlined in the system.

In general though, the more visible you are, the better.

Let me qualify this for a minute:

I'm not saying you should go out and buy a billboard next to the interstate... but if you're going to have a shop, and all other things are equal, you'd always be better off if your shop is visible, because people will know you're there.

This makes all your other campaigns and advertising work better.

Talk radio—

There are still some good talk radio stations out there. These are mostly located in larger cities. In general, ads for carpet cleaning on the radio don't pay for themselves. They are good for visibility, but you probably don't need to be trying to buy visibility from your local advertising rep.

Your advertising rep will probably strongly disagree with this, but you can't listen to them. They are in the business of selling advertising, and it's really in their best interest to sell things that aren't that track-able. That way there are no consequences for them.

I'm not saying that they are all a bunch of soulless pirates... but some of them are.

Carpet cleaners seem to like radio because they can hear their ads and it makes them feel 'big time'.

This is completely an ego stroke. I've had owners of carpet cleaning companies have their friends come up to them at parties and say, "I heard you on the radio the other day!"

The proper response to that question is, "Did you call in and buy anything?" The answer will be 'no'.

Talk radio can sometimes provide some decent results however. The only way this works is to get a celebrity endorsement from the host.

Remember, people that listen to talk radio are making a special effort to tune in to this person's show, so they value what he or she has to say.

So you have to have that very same person, the one with the relationship with the listeners, do the endorsement... not you.

You aren't nearly as believable as the host is... they don't trust you, because they don't know you.

This is something that you might want to do later on as you get bigger. I wouldn't advise adding it to the mix if you're small. When you're small, you probably need to be more targeted than radio can allow you to be.

RSVP–

RSVP is a company that has locally-owned franchises in most cities and towns of any size. Basically it's a card deck, that sends postcards out all together in a package to the upscale neighborhoods in a local area. (Think about it as a really nice, upscale version of val-pak.)

For a pretty reasonable price, you can have an incredible number of your postcards delivered to the neighborhoods that are probably full of prime candidates for your services.

This strategy can work well because the numbers are so large and the price is right.

You're mailing a postcard, so you've got to go with total direct-response as far as format. You want to tell your story as much as you can and make an offer with a deadline.

Over time, response rates can fall off a bit, which means that this is like anything else... You have to track the numbers to know where you stand.

Farming program–

This is a system where you take certain neighborhoods or areas and you basically lay siege to them for an extended period of time.

It looks like this: You'll pick an area that has maybe 300 homes in it and you'll do a mailing to that area every month or two. You'll explain what makes you unique and why you're the best choice for them. You'll drive the area in your van several times a week so that people can see you. You'll send them refrigerator magnets.

Every time you do a job in the area, you'll do the street mailing program to the whole area...

Your job is to make them think you're the only carpet cleaner in town, and that all of their neighbors are using you.

There is a general rule in advertising that in order to gain awareness in someone's mind, you have to make at least seven impressions within an eighteen-month period.

This is a long-term strategy, but it will help you to dominate the areas where your target market lives.

Other strategies–

There are many other things that you can try... the industry is full of them. Some of them sound good, but they don't really work very well. Some of them probably work very well. The key is to keep track of the results.

With proper tracking, you can easily figure out what's working and what isn't. The tracking is the key.

It's also very important that you test small before you throw a major chunk of your money at an idea. The idea will sound good to you and it will make perfect sense... but it still might not work. If it doesn't, you've blown your money and you'll have no results to show for it. Be careful of this, it can really create a problem for you. I've seen owners get so excited about a particular idea that they seem to lose all common sense.

Let me boil this down for you: Basically, you'd be far better off buying a tracking system, than buying a bunch of advertising strategies. This is true because the tracking system will show you what's working and what isn't. The strategies may work or they may not. They may work for a while, and then quit working. Without the tracking system, you'll never know.

That's why one of the main components in my marketing system is a system that will allow you to accurately track the results of whatever you're doing.

This isn't paint-by-numbers, it's business, and although there are useful strategies out there, you'll need to find the ones that work for you.

Other Promotional And Visibility Strategies

There are a few other things that reliably work to build a business. These are miscellaneous things that kind of form a base for the growth of the business.

In smaller companies, these are usually things that the owner does to promote the business. As the company grows, some of these functions will be taken over by employees.

There is no substitute for the owner or someone else getting out in the field and making sales.

This can be a formal effort, or it can be as simple as taking 20 business cards and not coming back until you've handed them out.

As your company grows you'll want to add a salesperson that does nothing else, but initially this will probably be you.

The employee that does sales needs a well-defined system, and you've got to be able to know what they are doing on a day-to-day basis, as well as the results of what they accomplished. This means a tracking system as well as a system to pay them for results.

What works best is a system of a combination of phone calls, mail, and in-person visits. This is a business-to-business sales system, that is similar to what is used by any company that is selling to businesses.

Your town probably has local networking groups. These groups meet weekly, are very structured, and exist for the sole purpose of referring leads for the members of the group.

There are many other opportunities to network. You will get business from being involved in, and visible in, any type of a group.

This could be a church, a service organization, city council... anything where you have a chance to interact with other people.

Another very useful thing to do is to develop referral relationships with other professionals that are in a position to refer work to you.

You'll use your standard referral program for this, where you pay them a referral fee, and you'd use this with rug retailers, carpet retailers, realtors, interior designers... just about anyone that has clients that they might be in a position to refer to you.

Often, these people are in the same boat you are when it comes to getting new business. They are often grateful when you refer people to them. Returning the favor goes a long way to building a relationship.

One last thing you can do to build your business is to use publicity. Publicity gives you authority as a specialist and it is very believable. People might not believe an ad that you wrote about yourself, but they will believe an article someone else wrote about you.

Several things of this type can be done... You could suggest that your local TV station do an exposé on bait and switch carpet cleaners in your area. You could do the same thing with a newspaper.

Occasionally, magazines will do an article on companies that advertise with them. I had one client have a feature article written about them in a women's magazine since the wife was half owner of the business, and the magazine was looking to do a piece on woman-owned businesses.

You'll have to look for publicity opportunities. One thing's for certain, magazines, newspapers, radio, and TV stations need material that is provocative and entertaining for their shows and articles... they have to write about something.

One client had a weekly column in the newspaper where people could ask questions and he'd answer them.

The possibilities are great, but you have to be a little creative and look for the opportunity.

Investing In Advertising

Let's say you have several good, proven strategies that you can use to grow your business... but you have no money to invest in advertising. You're sunk!

Oh sure, there are still things you can do, but you aren't going to be able to make massive headway towards building a million-dollar, level three company if you don't have any money to spend!

This is perhaps one of the biggest things that stops people from ever really getting off the ground as far as their advertising goes. What will happen is that owners will scrape together enough money to do some type of campaign, and then when the money comes back in, they'll spend it on other things.

Now of course no one means to do this, what they tell themselves is that they'll just pay these few bills right now... and then they'll set aside some money for future advertising from some money they'll be getting a little later on.

It could be later on in the day, later on in the week, or later on in the month... it doesn't really matter. What matters is that they aren't setting aside anything right now!

What too often happens, is that later on, things are a little slower than they had hoped and the money doesn't show up the way they thought it would.

Now they're back in the situation where they have no money for advertising again...

The way around this is to set aside a certain amount from every dollar that comes in. I'd recommend 10%.

If you take 10% right off the top, and commit to using that to build your business, you'll always have money to advertise with.

This is powerful because obviously if you don't re-invest, you can't grow.

This is how the large companies do it... They have a budget, and they set aside the money for advertising.

Obviously if things are tight, you might have to cut back. But you can't cut back on the one thing that's going to make your business grow!

This is an area that people fool themselves a lot in. They justify spending the money that should go to their company, and then they wonder why they can't get their company to grow.

This takes self-control and a tremendous amount of honesty to pull off. You may have to reduce your expenses or get out there and earn more money, but failing to do this will keep you small.

I have clients that regularly spend as much as $160,000 every month on advertising. That's a staggering amount of money every month. Chances are, you'll never get to a point where you'll need to spend anything near that, even if you build a million-dollar company. But you will have to spend much more than you are now if you're currently small.

The only way to get there is to start setting some aside... then, as you grow, you'll automatically have what you need when the time comes.

If you'll set aside 10%, you'll always be able to fund the advertising you need to grow your business.

You've now been given an overview of the sales system and the marketing system. These work, there's no question about it... But they'll only work to the degree they're implemented and tracked.

As the saying goes: You can't manage something you can't measure.

Most people start off with good intentions, but they soon get busy and often things slip.

What is needed is good management.

Management doesn't happen by accident. It takes strong systems and planning. You've got to be able to know that all of the critical areas in your business are handled, and that everything is being done exactly as you planned it. This is true whether you are doing a particular function yourself, or if you've delegated it to someone else.

In addition, management will set you free... it will provide the freedom to allow you to step away from your business and still have it accomplish what you want it to... even without your direct involvement.

Let's now explore the management system and I'll show you how this will allow you to make more money and be free.

10.

The Management System

There is a popular myth that small business owners have: They talk about someday in the future when they can hire a 'manager' to 'manage' their business, and then they'll be free.

This myth happens everywhere. The top salesman gets promoted, and now he's managing the sales department.

But the very things that make this person good at sales, probably make him a horrible candidate for a manager. Good salespeople aren't always the most organized, and details often fall through the cracks!

Business owners often talk about how they 'manage' their businesses...

But just what is management anyway?

Management is the control of a process or an organization. It also implies leading the organization somewhere, although that's really more about leadership.

When most small companies hire managers, and things go wrong, almost without exception the owner decides that the problem was the manager...

So, he fires the manager and tries to find a new, better one...Someone who 'gets it'.

The owner might be right... the old manager could have been absolutely terrible!

But almost never does the owner look at the actual management system.

In fact, there almost never is one!

What this owner is looking for is the perfect person… if only the perfect person would show up, then everything would be great!

The question is, how do you define the perfect person?

For most owners, it's someone exactly like them!

They want someone who will think the way they do, make the same decisions that they would in any given circumstance, and generally accomplish everything they would.

The problem is, most owners would never hire and never tolerate anyone that was exactly like themselves! They'd be fired before noon!

The point I'm trying to make here is that most people try to fix management problems by trying to find the right person.

But it's far easier, and far more effective, to set up well-designed and well-controlled management systems that anyone with a reasonable level of organization and focus could run.

This person now assumes the function of monitoring everything in the business. He makes sure that the smallest details are being done the way you want them to.

What's important though, is that this person reports to you on a weekly basis and proves it!

In our discussion of the management system, we're going to cover:

- The purpose of the management system– What it does and how it gives you freedom and control.

- The strategic planning process– Learn about a powerful process that aligns every key player in your company and holds them accountable for results.

- What it takes to manage your people– The concepts, key elements, and systems used to manage any employee in any function.

- Compensation strategies– How to get your employees to WANT to do what you want them to.

- An example of some of the critical areas in your business– These are the critical pulse-points that allow you to know what's going on and how well each person, each department, and the business as a whole is doing.

- An example of what the system typically looks like in an actual carpet cleaning company's on-location department

Most business owners think they can manage well. The truth is, no one can do a really great job of managing anything, without well-structured systems and a lot of definition.

This isn't a popular view. Most owners would much rather just keep winging it than take the time to build systems and accountabilities in their businesses.

And the truth is... most owners don't know how. They've never done it before.

Some owners have read books and understand the importance of having systems in their business... but the truth is, they don't even know what a system really looks like. What's in a system anyway? How is it built, and how is it managed? Do you know? Have you ever written out the systems for an entire company?

If you suspect you're probably not all that good at management, then you are just like some of the most successful and most respected business people in the world!

The fact is, most people that start businesses, and I'm not just talking carpet cleaners here... I mean all businesses, are good at directing... they are good at the vision...

But all the little details bore them to tears! It's probably not that they CAN'T do it... It's probably more that they HATE doing it! So guess what? They don't.

The problem is, this behavior will become a limit on the growth of the business at some point.

Systemizing a business can be one of the most profitable things you can ever do for a company. I know it doesn't seem like it would be, but it's true. It also removes an absolute set-in-stone, concrete limit, to how big and how successful the company can be.

Some companies are at that limit already, and some won't really be there for a while, but as you approach that limit, things start to not work as well. Efficiencies drop off. Problems multiply...chaos reigns supreme.

Hopefully this all doesn't sound too familiar to you.

What Is The Purpose Of The Management System?

There is another scenario that often happens with owners and managers.

Sometimes when the manager is hired, he comes in and acts as a CEO. He makes everything the way he wants it.

Well, that's obviously not going to work for you, the owner, if some manager has come in and set everything up in his own favor.

The manager has to be there to run the systems you set up. It just can't be any other way. The manager has input, sure, but ultimately you started this business to do something for YOU, so we need to make sure that the systems within your company, really reflect that goal.

Most people think that a business system is a written-down procedure.

It has to be much more than that if it is to really work in the real-world. It needs several components, and it can't just sit on the shelf... It needs to be incorporated into the day-to-day workings of the business.

This system and the principles behind it, help you do just that... to really get the systems working, and above all else, accurately measured in the real-world.

The system allows you to control all of the critical areas of your business—all the areas we've been talking about... sales, production, and marketing.

With this control, comes the ability to direct and change course. If you don't like the direction things are taking, you can change it.

Without this control, you can have all of the pieces and things will still fall apart.

If you're trying to build an empire, I can tell you that building a self-sustaining, million-dollar business that runs seamlessly without you being there is no small feat! THAT'S a real trick to pull off, and in order to do it, you're going to need a lot more control over every aspect of your business than you probably have right now.

This is the part where most people fall down. They don't have a way to really take control of everything they need to in order to build their business.

And with all this talk of building million-dollar companies... let's not forget that you absolutely need that control even if you're much smaller than that.

This is a very common 'hidden' reason for a lot of struggle in our industry. Until you realize this, it becomes impossible to build your business past a certain point.

Maybe you've had that problem.

You simply can't manage something you can't measure.

Another way of saying that is, if you won't measure it, you'll never be able to manage it.

The marketing and sales systems are amazing, and what they can do for your company will amaze you! But without management, they won't get used!

I've seen this time and time again, even in large companies where there are many people that are managers.

Without meaning to, they fall off the system and quit using it.

Let me put it bluntly. Without the management system, there is no way any of the other systems will work long-term.

The management system is the thing that allows you to be free of the business. It is a system that allows you to walk away and still have control over what's going on while you're not there.

It allows you to have a manager that is checking on everything, and you know that manager is aware of what is happening in the business, and most importantly, there is a path for that knowledge of what's going on… to get back to you.

The management system gives you the freedom and the ability to control every aspect of your business. Basically, what has to happen in order for this to be true, is that you have to design and define every element within your business and then set up systems to monitor the results. This is a lot of work. Thankfully I've done most of it for you.

What Happens In A Business With No Structure

Businesses without clearly defined structure are incredibly inefficient. This is why sometimes implementing a system that really allows you to control what's going on inside your business can be one of the most profitable things you can do for your business.

Another thing that almost always happens without management, is that your customers get an inconsistent message and experience from your various employees and salespeople. This leads to customer confusion and sometimes outright hostility.

I'm sure you've dealt with a situation where the customer was understandably upset because they were told something they shouldn't have been, and now they're expecting something that you can't deliver.

That's a worst-case scenario, but what commonly happens, in fact it probably happens every day in a company with a few employees, is that the sales message is inconsistent and the results are unpredictable.

That's why some people seem to be able to sell really well, and it's easy for them, and others struggle and can't seem to get anywhere close to the result of the sales superstars.

Have you ever wondered why your employees can't seem to sell as well as you do? They don't have a consistent method that is controlled for doing it.

The same thing happens with the quality of the cleaning. It's very easy for technicians to pretty much do whatever they feel like doing out there in the field, and in most cases, no one will ever know. That's just got to make you a little nervous... especially since if anything goes wrong, you're the one that's going to have to buy the customer a replacement!

Now it's possible that you spend a lot of time and probably a lot of money training your technicians. (If you don't have technicians yet... you almost certainly will at some point, and if you follow these systems, it will probably be soon.)

But training alone won't guarantee behavior. That is probably one of the biggest sources of frustration that small business owners have… they tell their employees to do something a certain way, and they come back a few weeks or a few months later and they aren't doing it that way at all!

I hate to tell you this, but the real responsibility for making sure your employees do things the right way is none other than yours! And you do that by either hovering over everyone's shoulder and driving them crazy… or you implement strong, effective management systems within your business.

Employees aren't accountable for results if there is not a clear-cut way to hold them accountable. This means accurate measurement of every meaningful result that is produced within a department or by a particular employee working in a position.

If this is starting to sound a little overwhelming, don't let that rattle you. It's actually easier than it sounds once it's all set up, and paradoxically, if you detest this kind of thing, it means you need it even more!

Without structure, there is no consistency of service. The methods used will not be the same from technician to technician.

There also are no clearly defined standards that everyone is held to. Now, again, sometimes owners have a problem with this concept because they tell their employees repeatedly exactly what is expected of them. But in any organization there are two realities.

First, there is what is said… this is what the owner wants to happen.

Second, there is what everyone can get away with… this is what REALLY happens!

Without a structure to track and measure every critical area at least weekly, things will inevitably drift and very quickly the inmates will be running the asylum!

One of the worst consequences of not having clear management and structure is the fact that at some point, the business will self-limit and further growth becomes impossible.

I have worked with many very large carpet cleaning companies. These companies have management, and often several layers of it. The managers that work in these companies are often college-educated with degrees in business and in management. These businesses are quite large, but many times they have quit growing… and no one can figure out why.

Whatever the structure of a business is... that structure has a limit.

The business can't grow beyond that structure.

If the business is to grow, then the structure must be changed.

This whole book and the three systems described here, are designed to do one thing: To get you to a place where you can be a level-three company with over a million dollars in revenue each year.

Now, if you decide that you want to be a level-four company and start having departmental managers and go on to multi-million dollar levels in gross receipts, I can show you how to do that… but your structure will have to change or it won't be possible.

So, to recap this, the purpose of the management system is:

√ To control the production and quality within the company
√ To control the sales and the sales process between your company and your customers
√ To control the marketing and to be able to track the effectiveness of the marketing so that you can control growth

If there is no structure:

X Your company is inefficient
X Your customers get an inconsistent sales message
X Your customers get inconsistent quality
X Your employees are not accountable for results
X There are no clearly defined standards and consequences
X The business will self-limit it's growth at some point

How To Achieve Goals With Your Company

Don't do it all yourself. As your company approaches a larger level two, you can begin to use the strategic planning process.

The strategic planning process is a process that gets buy-in from all of your employees and supervisors, and it also educates them so that ultimately they are able to take over the day-to-day operations of the business.

This should be done early on in the growth of your company, because it gets everyone used to the process and teaches them how to hit pre-determined goals.

Here's how it works and what it looks like:

Objectives–

You meet with all of your managers or supervisors, or people that are in charge of the various parts of your company. What you do is TOGETHER, you pick a company goal for the following year. This goal should include things like gross revenue, gross profit, sales goals for various people or departments, average job size, etc.

Plan of action for each department–

Now I realize you may not have departments in your company, but the same principle holds true even if you're managing individuals. Each person has to commit to making their piece of the puzzle happen.

In other words, the group and the individual have to agree that in order to hit the big goal, that each person has to achieve a specific smaller goal for their department or area.

Each person has to agree that the goal is reasonable, but the others have to hold this person accountable for not taking the easy way out as well. If a certain person doesn't feel that they can accomplish a certain outcome, either the big goal needs to be changed, or maybe you have the wrong person in that position.

Each person develops a plan of action that includes what they are going to do if it looks like they are falling short of the goal. (You may have to help them with their plans...)

Plans are presented to the group–

Now, each person presents their plan to the group by the individuals that are responsible for each department or area.

In addition to the plan, each person should have contingency plans... that is, what they are going to do if it looks like they are starting to miss their milestones.

In other words, how will they get back on track?

Pick measurements that will show progress–

Now, you have to pick specific measurements that are as objective as possible to show if the person is on track for hitting their part of the goal. These measurements will be given during a monthly meeting with all members of the strategic planning group.

What this does is use the group to help hold each individual accountable for their results.

Incorporate the plan into the job descriptions–

Now, you make sure that the plan itself, and the measurements are included in each person's job description which you will be scoring weekly. This makes certain that all of the key people are working the problem and they know that you are monitoring their progress.

Adjust as needed—

Things change, and sometimes you find that a goal that everyone thought was quite reasonable, just isn't going to happen in the time frame everyone was thinking it would. That's perfectly fine. Just set a new time frame, or revise the goal... or get everyone to take additional action to make the goal happen.

Goals are moving targets, the important thing is that you have a process that gets the most out of the people that are leading your various departments.

You are also teaching what will ultimately be your management team, how to pick a target and work toward getting it. This process along with some of the others, becomes your basis for personal freedom.

What It Takes To Manage Your People

Let's talk about what it really takes to manage your people. And what I'm really talking about here is how you manage a process. Your business isn't composed of people that you manage... it's composed of processes that you manage.

In order to manage pretty much anyone or any department, you need two things:

1. Communication
2. Enforcement

Communication is where you tell everyone what's expected. You clearly set out the deal. You tell them in explicit detail, exactly how to win the game.

Enforcement sounds like something the Gestapo would do, but it's really not. All enforcement means, is that you have some system of checking the results so you can measure if people are doing what they are supposed to or not.

If you don't have clear communication, then it becomes impossible for people to really know what you mean for them to do. They won't be able to succeed because they have to go through a trial and error process in order to find out what you really meant.

Most owners don't think this is a problem. But if you go in to almost any company as I do, as a third party, and interview the owner, and ask about a certain position, you'll get one viewpoint about what that job consists of.

However, if you interview the person actually doing the job, about 80 to 90% of the time, you'll get a completely different answer. We're not talking about subtle interpretations here, we're talking about two completely different jobs. These are often worlds apart.

The communication provides an alignment of purpose between all the parties so everyone is on the same page.

The enforcement portion of this isn't a strict performance review or disciplinary action… it's more like coaching.

It's almost like the owner says, "Let's see how you're doing." And then there is a discussion about how things could be done better.

There will always be things that could be worked on or improved, and so you'll pick one or two items that the employee should work on during the following week and you'll both agree on what actions should be taken and how the employee is to proceed. This whole process is usually friendly and supportive. If it's not, you've probably got the wrong person in one of the positions.

(Keep in mind that one of the positions is you!)

All of this is written down and signed by you and the employee, and then the next week, you basically say, "Let's see how you're doing." And it all goes from there.

Dan Kennedy (no relation, by the way...) tells a story about a famous loss-prevention consultant. He worked with big retail stores and he was one of the very best. He was in high demand.

When he would start working with someone, he'd explain his philosophy about people.

"Five percent of the people will ALWAYS steal." He'd say.

"Another five percent will NEVER steal."

"And the remaining ninety percent will steal, if they have three things:

1. If they feel like they have a need for the item.
2. If they have the opportunity to take it.
3. If they have the belief that they'll get away with it.

If you take away one of these three, then you'll eliminate theft ninety-five percent of the time... and the other five percent you can't do anything about."

Now I suppose this doesn't say anything very good about human nature, but it does raise an interesting point.

If this guy is right, and he quite possibly is... then it means that most people will take advantage of you if given the need... the opportunity... and the belief that they'll get away with it.

Now I'm not talking about someone embezzling money from your company. But what I am talking about is little things... cutting corners, not really doing what they should, or obeying the letter of the law but not the spirit of it.

Or it may not even be as blatant as that. The point I'm making is that if you don't check on people, you're being pretty naïve if you think that they're going to do things the way you told them because they ought to.

Human nature doesn't really work that way. People take shortcuts. People know that there is the way management wants it done... and then there's the real world way of getting things done.

If this scares you a little, you're not alone. When you get right down to it, this is the problem that keeps a lot of small business owners from growing.

These are the 'employee headaches' that no one wants to mess with.

Because very few people have found a way around it. Very few people have a way that works.

What I'm telling you is that this system will give you control over that.

Nearly everyone knows they should systemize their business. The problem is, most people wouldn't know a system if it bit them on the rear!

So just what is a system anyway?

Well, a system is a written-down procedure... the problem is, it's much more than that too.

One of the most necessary components of a system is something called a feedback loop.

A feedback loop is just a way for information to get back to the people that have an ability to affect it.

In other words you tell people how they're doing and give them information as to how they could do better.

Now that sounds simple enough when you say it like that... but the truth is, most companies are absolutely horrible at this. Usually people get so reactive, that they are always at the mercy of what's happening, instead of being pro-active where they are at the cause of what's happening.

So what is needed is a way to take that critical information and feed it back to the people doing the work.

That's the system that is needed, and in just a few more pages, I'll tell you exactly how to do it.

This feedback allows you to try something and then measure the results... then, you're able to try something else and measure the results of that.

This gives you and every person in your company a way to continuously improve performance.

Elements Of A Job Description

All of the systems within the company should reside within the job descriptions of the people working there.

When you think about it, where else should they be? The difference is, these aren't traditional job descriptions.

Most job descriptions are really lists of duties and responsibilities. They usually fit on one or two sheets of paper. They almost never tell how anything is supposed to be done or to what standard... they just say that certain things are supposed to be done. This feeds right into the problem of interpretation of the job that I talked about earlier.

If one person thinks something should be done one way, and another person thinks things ought to be done some other way, who is right?

Obviously the owner has the right to call the shots here, but in most cases, the owner thinks that the method to follow is obvious.

And so both people work along... never realizing that there is a problem until something critical happens that shows that the employee and the owner or manager really aren't on the same page at all!

The other thing that happens with job descriptions is that they are generally only looked at during the hiring process. After the person is hired, they are filed and forgotten about.

Maybe they come out of the file during some disciplinary process, but other than that, people generally operate on the 'if it ain't broke, don't fix it', theory.

A job description can be and should be so much more than that. It can help you to manage your people in ways you probably wouldn't believe.

First off, it can be the training manual for the job.

If it includes more than just a list of duties and responsibilities... if it also includes HOW to do the things, it becomes much more valuable. Now, it's a yardstick for performance... especially if it includes how things are to be measured. (Which, of course, it has to!)

In other words, what exactly defines a good job? What defines the minimum acceptable job... and what isn't nearly good enough? How will these things be measured, and what will the consequences be?

Who will take the measurements and how often?

Now, imagine what happens when all of these elements are defined and there is a scheduled meeting where a manager or supervisor gives each employee the feedback on how well they are doing their job.

What happens now is all the employees know exactly what's expected of them. They know that the manager or owner is checking and checking regularly. They know that there are consequences if they fail to hit the minimum acceptable level of performance in all the critical areas for that job.

There are also good consequences if they exceed expectations, but they never get the chance to decide that the management is asleep at the wheel and doesn't know what's really going on.

This method is how you take control of a company. It will allow you to change the culture inside your company, as well as measure and control each critical aspect of your organization, from the top all the way down to the bottom.

This will make you money.
This will get you free
This will give you control.

Some owners hear this and a light goes on. They say, "Of course... It's so obvious! That sounds great!"

But others protest.

They talk about how much work it will be and they talk about how they don't want to mess with the details.

If you don't take care of the details in your business, who will? And if you allow someone else to do it, how will you make sure you get what you want?

This does take some work, but the payoff is huge!

It's organization, it's structure... and the truth is, some business owners don't see themselves as that kind of a person. They'd much rather go through life by the seat of their pants. After all, that's what's gotten them this far.

Well, that may be, the problem is, it won't take them where they need to go. It's really as simple as this:

If you don't take control of your business, then you will have an uncontrolled business!

You will always be wondering why there is so much chaos in your life, and the answer will be that it's coming from your uncontrolled business!

Besides, it's really not all that hard to do. It takes time, but it is one of the best investments in time that you could ever make.

And of course, you could always buy the systems from me. If you do, it contains everything you need, pre-built! You just modify it to fit your business, if you need to at all, and you're up and running.

Keep in mind that the large, super-successful companies that I worked with, did not build their systems themselves… No, they hired an expert (me) to build those systems for them.

In the end, it doesn't really matter where you get your systems from, as long as you get the systems running in your business and it gives you control. You have to go for the result in this case, and it truly doesn't matter how you get there… as long as you do.

Now, I have to say that any systems you buy, need to have certain critical components. If they don't, they'll be incomplete.

There are a few people out there selling 'systems' for the carpet cleaning industry. The problem is, they are mostly just written-down procedures, and a written-down procedure is NOT a system. It won't give you any real control over anything!

So lets take a look at what needs to be inside a job description to really make it work as a system for you.

What you need are six key things:

1. Purpose And Vision– This is where you explain your company's vision and what you're trying to do. You give the employee a vision for how they are supposed to do their job.

You paint a picture for them of what it is you want them to do and what's in it for them... and what's in it for you.

There is nothing wrong with being a little idealistic here. You want to sell them on your vision. This is what they're buying into when they take the job.

2. Why The Job Is Necessary– This is where you tell the employee how their position fits in with the other members of the team. They need to have an overall picture so that they understand why the job is critical and why they need to do things in the way that you're asking them.

This may seem like it's unnecessary. After all, you're paying the bills, and they ought to do things the way you want them to without a lot of explaining on your part, right?

Well, of course... but when employees understand the big picture, they understand in a better way what you're trying to accomplish. When they know that, they can actually do a better job of helping you accomplish YOUR goals.

In many ways, the Purpose And Vision, and Why The Job Is Necessary, are some of the most critical elements of the job description, because together, they lead to an alignment and understanding of purpose between the employee and the management.

3. Duties And Responsibilities– This is where you give them the traditional list of things you want them to do for your company. This is pretty standard, no surprises here.

It's interesting to note that this is the ONLY thing included in most job descriptions. It's almost like people are afraid of too much detail.

4. Operational Definition– This is where you tell them exactly HOW you want them to do the job you're asking them to do. How are things to be done, and to what level.

This is where the job description really gets it's richness and depth. This portion of the job description can be used as an outline for training.

You don't have to tell them about every micro-detail, but you at least need to outline exactly how things are to be done. You'd cover things like how, when, where, with what... you get the idea.

5. Personal Characteristics Required To Succeed– In other words, what kind of person makes a good fit for this kind of position. This is very useful during the hiring process.

If you had to describe the type of person that would be successful in this job, what type of person would they be. Now it's true, that you may already have people working in these positions right now that you've already found... but remember, we're setting things up so that SOMEONE ELSE can do this FOR you at some point. At some time in the future, someone's going to need to know this, so let's build it now, and you can get yourself free!

In addition to describing the person ideally suited for this position, this is where we describe the working environment of the job itself.

6. Performance Criteria– These are how we measure performance. In other words, we ask the question, "If this job were being done in an excellent manner… what would be true?"

Ideally, the performance criteria should be measures on every critical area of the job, and they should be as objective as possible so they are not open to interpretation by the employee, the manager, or anyone else.

They should just result in a measurement of performance.

Performance criteria might be things like average job size, revenue per hour, re-do percentage, average up-sell amount, and so forth.

You don't want to have 50 measurements here, although the higher up the chain the job is, in general, the more measurements of performance you'll need. But in any case, you want to have as few measurements as possible, but you need to be able to get a good read on performance from those measurements. For most jobs, you'll probably have between five and ten measurements.

These measurements will tell you and the employee, what kind of job the employee is doing… however, the performance criteria concept is almost useless without consequences, both good and bad as a result of performance or lack of performance.

If you have those critical items, you have taken care of the communications side of the job. The employee and you, will know exactly what is expected of anyone holding this position.

But there is one last critical element that we need in order to really be able to take control of the job. What is still missing?

Enforcement.

The Weekly One-On-One Meetings

A weekly one-on-one meeting is a forum where the EMPLOYEE comes in and tells YOU how they are doing their job. Of course they have to prove it… they can't just come in and tell you things are great when they're not!

It works best when the employee comes in with the figures that you are using to measure him or her by. This trains the employee to look at and be aware of those figures.

In most cases, you will both be showing up with some measures.

You review each of the critical measures found under the 'Performance Criteria' section of the job description with the employee, and you pick an area for the employee to work on during the following week. You write all of this down on the employee's performance criteria review form. This form acts as a scorecard for the employee and communicates how they are doing. (Feedback loop)

The very act of holding this meeting is the enforcement part of the equation.

The meetings have the feel of a coaching session, although if strong disciplinary actions are called for, you can certainly take them during this meeting.

Everything is written down… the praise… the critiques… the actions the employee agrees to take during the following week to correct any problems or just to improve their performance.

The form is signed by both you and the employee, and it is filed until the following week.

These one-on-one meetings should not take that long. About 10 minutes is pretty typical if you're meeting with a technician. If you're meeting with a salesperson or a manager, it might take longer to go over everything. (This meeting shouldn't take that long to do, however.)

How The Weekly One-On-One Meetings Are Used In A Company Structure

The idea is to have a weekly one-on-one with every person in the company each week… but this follows a pyramid-style management structure.

In other words, when you start to have quite a few people working in your company, a mid-level manager will hold the weekly one-on-ones with all of their subordinates, and then this manager will report to you.

In cases where the owner is not really there at the company any more and the entire show is being run by a general manager, the weekly one-on-one with the general manager can take some time. You'll probably want to allow about an hour for that meeting, but at the end of the meeting, you'll know exactly where every person stands throughout your entire company. Pretty powerful, huh?

So every key measure throughout the company is taken once per week and then transmitted upward.

This is how you get yourself free. You step away, but you don't give up the control. You have a clearly defined system that gets followed even when you're not there, and you check on every critical area every week.

So, you're not there, but you know that:

- the vans were inspected
- the sales training meeting was held
- in-field inspections were made on all technicians
- you know the average job size for each technician
- all of the critical sales measures for each technician
- you know the person answering the phone was monitored
- you know the advertising is on track
- you know which employees were warned, and if there were any problems
- And anything else YOU decide is critical!

You know all of this, and you weren't even there this week! What's more, you have seen the documentation that proves that everything is true.

If you're out of town, you can hold this meeting over the web using video conferencing.

AND YOU'RE STILL GETTING PAID FROM THE BUSINESS!

This is why you own a business... not so you can work your tail off 80 hours a week!

Please understand: You'll have to work hard... It's one of the requirements for success, but you shouldn't have to do it forever.

A final benefit is the organization that this brings. A common occurrence is that an employee repeatedly violates some provision in their job, and sometimes this employee must be let go.

The problem is, almost no one ever documents the employees' lack of performance. So if there is ever an issue where the department of labor must get involved, the owner often loses because he or she can't prove that any violation ever occurred, or that anyone ever gave the employee any warning about it.

Think about the strong position you'd be in if you could show repeated violations every week, on a form that you and the employee signed!

The difference between the two is night and day.

The Compensation Game

There probably isn't a single tool that can help you get control of your people more than the way you pay them.

Almost everyone knows that performance-based pay works, but almost everyone is very unsophisticated about it.

Let's look at some various types of pay structures and examine the pros and cons of each one.

There really are only a few different ways to pay people for their work.

You can maybe best look at this as a game. Each different way of paying people results in a different way to play the game to win.

Hourly–

First of all, we have the tried-and-true hourly pay. This pay system is easy, and that's why many people use it.

From the employees' selfish interest, the employee wins this game by taking longer to do a job. There is always the possibility of overtime if the employee works extra hours, so there is a reward for slowing down.

The employee will often clock in at the first possible second, and many times will spend 15 or 20 minutes getting coffee, going to the restroom... and generally anything else that needs to be done before getting down to the business of work.

At the end of the day the process is reversed. The employee may have their car loaded and started before actually clocking out.

Under this pay structure you are paying people for being clocked in and 'on-the-job', so that's what you get.

An employee 'wins' this game by staying clocked in as long as possible.

Salary–

In a salary pay situation, things are almost reversed. Here, the employee gets paid a fixed amount of money, regardless of time spent or results achieved.

For the employee to 'win' under this type of pay structure, the employee needs to produce results, but only those results that are necessary to avoid raising an alarm.

In other words, the employee usually does the barest minimum.

Many times, salaried employees will get by with coming in a little late, and leaving a little early. They aren't paid to be there for a certain number of hours, and so they usually aren't.

The employee often justifies this behavior by pointing out the times that they worked late or were on call. However, in most cases, if the owner really knew the number of times they worked late, versus the number of times they leave early, the owner usually wouldn't feel like the employee is doing enough.

Commission–

Very few employees will accept a pure commission job, because a pure commission pay structure lacks security, which is a basic human need.

The truth is, most people don't have the resources to go even two weeks without a pay check. This is why you can explain the benefits of a commission pay system to most employees, and they will still turn it down.

A true salesperson, however, will always opt for a commission pay structure, because they have confidence in their ability to produce and they know that they'll make more by participating in a piece of the action, than by settling for a safer, more secure, but less lucrative pay structure.

You might say that the salesperson's confidence in their own ability to produce a result IS the security they need from their job.

Commission pay structures have many advantages, but it is difficult to get employees to accept the fact that they never know for sure what they are going to get paid.

Combinations–

In just about any business system, you are going to have positives and negatives. Very seldom, if ever, do you come across a system that has all of the advantages you want with none of the disadvantages.

When you start to combine pay structures however, it is possible to end up with a structure that often gives you most of what you want without too many disadvantages.

Compensation Produces Behavior

The reason that compensation is so powerful is that it really does produce behavior. A good compensation plan can actually get your people working WITH you by harnessing the employees' natural desire to act in their own selfish interest.

The employees will still act in their own self-interest, but a good compensation plan will align their self-interest with your own.

I was doing a two-day training for some call-center personnel in Dallas many years ago.

I was just starting out as a consultant, and what we'd done was split the call-center personnel into two groups. The owner of the company wanted to see the results of my training, and then if the program worked, he would agree to train the rest of the call center.

About every two hours we'd take a break. The call-center personnel, who were all women, would stand outside the training room and a few of them would smoke, and they'd talk, and after 15 or 20 minutes, we'd resume the class.

These women were paid hourly. Part of my program was to convert them to a commission-based pay structure.

I bet them a steak dinner at Del Frisco's that once they had tried the commission pay structure, they'd never want to go back!

Well, I won the bet... (I didn't make them pay me) but what was interesting was what happened a few months later.

You'll remember my deal with the owner of the company– if the program was successful, he'd have me back in to train the rest of his people.

Well, two months later the results were in, the program was a success, and I was back, training the other half of the call center. Same kind of group... all women...

So the first day, we got going and things were going well, and it was time to take our first break, so we did... only problem was, when it was time to start the training again... the women were nowhere to be found!

I asked around, but no one had seen them. I began to worry that maybe I had given them the impression that we were done! Maybe they had gone home!

Finally I walked across the property to the main office where the call center was located and where their manager was.

Guess where the women all were?...

They were in the office... ON THE PHONES!!!

They were taking calls.

Working!

I finally got them all rounded up and as we were walking back down to the training facility, I heard one of the women say to another, "I just made 40 bucks!"

So we have vastly different behavior, all because of the pay structure.

The first time I did the training, the women were paid hourly, and they were quite happy to stand around, smoke, and get paid for it.

During the second training, it was like the break was on THEIR time! There was money to be made, and they got right to work. No one told them to... I guess they'd rather make 40 bucks than stand around and smoke!

My point is that compensation really does produce behavior and when you get your employees' selfish interests aligned with the interests of your company, then everyone is working together and pulling in the same direction.

This reduces the need for intensive management, since to some degree, people start managing themselves.

A Real-World Example

What I'd like to do is to give you a real-world example of a compensation structure that works.

There are a couple of variations on this, and I have companies that use a few different versions of this, but this structure is the core.

This pay structure is for carpet cleaning technicians:

Base Percentage–

The base percentage pay is 13%. The technician gets 13% of any job he or she does.

In addition to this base percentage, the technician is eligible for four additional bonuses, each of which raises the percentage he or she is able to get from the job.

Meeting Participation Bonus–

This is a bonus of 1% that is paid based on participation in the sales meeting and the production meeting. The technician can't be late and must participate in the meeting. This includes being able to give the sales presentation in the sales meeting, and presenting topics during the production meeting.

Van Inventory / Cleanliness Bonus–

This is a bonus of 1% that is paid provided that all items are accounted for in the technician's van and all equipment is clean and presentable.

This also covers personal appearance... the technician shouldn't come in for work with holes in his or her clothes or unshaven etc.

Procedure / Check Ride / Paperwork Bonus–

This is a bonus of 1% that is paid when the technician is using the sales presentation, uses a staging area for his job, and properly completes paperwork in full and on time

Platinum / Gold Percentage Bonus–

This is an added incentive to use the sales system. If a technician attempts to sell at all, he will easily sell at least 60% of the residential jobs at a platinum or a gold level.

The Platinum / Gold Percentage Bonus is a 1% bonus that is paid when the technician sells platinum and/or gold packages at a 60% level or greater.

Quality Measure Bonus–

This is a bonus that is paid for quality.

When it comes to quality, our perception of quality doesn't really matter. The person whose perception we need to worry most about, is the perception of the customer.

Also, anytime you pay someone on a commission, it becomes very easy for them to slip into what I call 'production mentality'.

Production mentality is where they figure out that they get paid a percentage of the work they get done each day, and instead of trying to sell more, they decide to try and win the game by blasting through as many jobs, as quickly as they possibly can!

This leads to high dollar amounts in production... but terrible quality!

Obviously no one's going to pay you top dollar for lousy service... they may do it once, but they'll never do it again!

The technicians qualify for this bonus by having an extremely low redo (or re-service) percentage.

Typically in order to qualify for this 2% Bonus, they have to have a redo percentage of less than 2 or 3%, over the last eight weeks. This keeps quality high, because you are paying them for it!

This bonus is big enough to make a difference

$10 per week Bonus–

It can be very frustrating when you buy your technicians new equipment and it gets lost or damaged because of carelessness.

Sometimes, also because of carelessness or because of taking shortcuts, things can be damaged during the cleaning process. Anyone who has had employees can absolutely count on having to replace things that were damaged during cleaning, at least a few times...

This $10 per week bonus is a powerful way to get people to pay attention to things like these.

The bonus works like this: Beginning on the first of the year, each week that goes by where nothing has been damaged and no equipment has been lost, you'll put $10 into a special bonus account for that technician. At the end of the year, you will give the technician the money. (You can actually give out the money two weeks before the year is up, and that will come in very handy for Christmas... So you're actually running this for 50 weeks out of the 52 weeks in a year.

The technician gets the money... PROVIDED there have been no damages to items he cleaned, and PROVIDED there has been no equipment lost during the year.

If something was damaged, or something was lost, then you'll take the cost of that item, out of the money that the technician has been building up.

It can be a tricky thing to take money out of someone's check. Making them personally responsible for items can be hard, and the employee can sometimes take it up with the department of labor. If you don't do this just right, it can blow up in your face.

This system is elegant, because the money is all coming out of a bonus... NOT out of the employee's pay! All you are doing is using whether or not items were missing or things were damaged to determine the amount of the bonus at the end of the year... however, you don't owe the employee any bonus at all. That is paid completely based on your discretion... but the employee still wants the money.

This means that since it is a bonus, it is above the laws pertaining to employee pay. The employee can never say that you didn't pay him... you just might not pay him an extra bonus! (Check with your attorney about this)

All of these bonuses and strategies will go a very long way toward making the employee want to do what you want them to... having said that, you are still on the hook for proper management.

You still need to provide feedback and enforcement of policies and procedures… it's just that with this pay structure, it becomes much easier to do because you won't have to do it nearly as much!

The employee, by working for their own selfish interest, inadvertently is working for YOUR interest as well!

The Critical Measures In Your Business

In order to have any sort of real control over your business, you have to be able to know where you stand. This, of course, takes measurement as well.

Many people would like to measure the critical areas of their businesses, but they aren't really sure what those critical areas are, and they aren't really sure how to set up systems to measure them.

This really isn't all that hard once you know how to do it. In fact, you do this the very same way that you set up measurements for each employee.

In that case, we were looking at performance criteria for a certain job or position, and we asked the question, "If this job were being done well… what would be true?"

You could easily ask the same question about a department.

What is needed, are critical measurements that get looked at every week, for literally every crucial area of the business.

What you'll find is that you are then able to look at the numbers and know exactly where any problems are within your whole company.

What's more, you'll catch those problems while they are still small, because you'll actually see them start to develop. You'll actually see the numbers start to slip and you'll be able to react to whatever situation you are confronted with, long before it reaches a crisis point.

The management system must do a couple of things. It has to show you what to measure... and you have to know what those measurements mean... in other words, you have to be able to take a certain measurement... but you also have to know what that measurement SHOULD be in the first place. Otherwise how will you know when something's wrong?

For instance, to measure a carpet cleaning technician, you need to know the following:

- The platinum and gold percentage
- The average job size
- The revenue per hour for the week
- The up-sell percentage
- The re-service percentage over the last eight weeks
- The total production figure for the week
- Add-on percentage
- Total Add-up amount
- Total square feet cleaned each day

If you know this information, you will know exactly how well that technician is doing. But there is still one problem...

What if no one in your company has ever done a great job at selling... or at providing quality service?

In other words, what will you compare these numbers to?

In the management system, I not only give you the critical measures, but I'll tell you what they should be in order to put you on a par with the best companies in the country!

Ultimately, the result of all of this is that you have the information you need to make the right call.

Without this information, you're gambling... you're taking chances, and you'll never really know if you're right or not.

With this information, things become controllable, predictable, manageable.

There is one other interesting thing that business owners sometimes do... and you should be on the lookout for it.

Sometimes, business owners don't want to know this information because they are afraid of the answer.

It's like asking someone for criticism. Many people would rather have no feedback at all, than have negative feedback!

This shows up in different ways. One of the most common, is when there is an employee that deep down, the owner knows, isn't really cutting it, but they don't want to confront the employee for some reason.

They may just like the person... or maybe they can't imagine their business without this person.

This person has become a sacred cow.

Sometimes an owner will basically make a choice to stick their head in the sand and ignore something, instead of measuring it, because then they'd have to do something about it.

Many times, an owner would rather tell themselves that things are fine, rather than face the fact that there are some problems that really require their attention.

The problem with this is obvious... you can't fix something you won't admit. Also, you won't know if the actions you're taking are bringing you closer to, or further away from where you want to go if you don't measure results.

An Overview Of The Management System For A Typical On-Location Cleaning Department

What I want to do in this section is give you some idea of what all of this looks like in the real world. In other words, I'd like to give you a 'tour' here, in words, of a department in a company that is using this system.

The vans are inspected on a random basis in the mornings. There is usually an on-location supervisor that does this.

The on-location supervisor is a low-level manager that also works a regular crew, but is in charge of the other technicians.

The on-location supervisor uses a checklist and checks the vans for safety items, equipment, chemicals, and also checks to make sure proper maintenance is done.

All of this is noted on several checklists.

These checks are done so that every van is checked at least once a week.

There are two early morning meetings held each week, a production meeting and a sales meeting.

During the production meeting, the technicians take turns giving a 5 to 10 minute presentation from a rotating list of about 20 topics. Each week a different technician presents on another of the topics. In addition, any problem areas are discussed. This keeps a focus on the actual mechanics of the cleaning and helps to remind the technicians about the processes to do a good job.

The sales meeting is similar in that each technician takes turns giving the presentation while the other technicians score the presentation on the calibration sheets.

After the presentation, which is done in a role-play format, everyone discusses the results they got and makes suggestions for improvement. This is also a time to share answers to objections and success stories.

When the technicians do a job, they follow a certain procedure, using the sales system. They unload their equipment into a staging area on the front porch or just inside the home.

The on-location supervisor stops by and does an in-field quality control check on each technician at least once a week. The results of these checks are written on a form.

As the technician finishes their day, they come back to the shop and ready the van for the next day's work. This includes washing the van on a scheduled basis, refilling the van with fuel, topping off all chemical containers and emptying and cleaning filters, etc.

The technician turns in the work orders from the day along with a daily transmittal form that shows exactly what the figures were for that technician for the day.

At the end of the week, the information from the daily forms is entered onto a weekly form for each technician.

On a scheduled, weekly basis, the on-location supervisor holds a weekly one-on-one meeting with each technician.

All figures from the week's work are reviewed with the technician. This includes things like average job size, amount of up-sells, platinum and gold percentage, etc.

Any items that need to be addressed are addressed during this meeting, and goals are set for the following week. The on-location supervisor and the technician both sign the weekly one-on-one report form.

Again, on a scheduled basis, the on-location supervisor meets with the owner or general manager and reports all key measures for his department.

The owner or general manager checks over the paperwork from the week... the on-location supervisor brings it all... checklists from the van, reports from the in-field checks, notes from the meetings.

In about half an hour to an hour, the owner or general manager knows for a fact exactly how every person within the on-location department is doing.

He knows that the check-rides were done, he knows who is giving the presentation and who is not. He knows who participated in the meetings, and he knows all of the critical measures for the entire department.

The owner or general manager, and the on-location supervisor pick goals for the following week and the owner or general manager is done!

I think you can maybe begin to see how this process can be used to manage a person... a department... or an entire company.

This is how you do it...

This is how you get there.

This is the only way to keep control of it all. It's organized, it's structured, it's efficient, and it works!

It can make you rich and set you free.

Every employee is working under a structure and every structure is designed to fill a purpose and to work with all of the other structures.

11.
Final Call To Action...

Much earlier on in this book, I talked about the levels of success concept... about how there are four levels of carpet cleaning companies.

Assuming you decide to become a million-dollar, level three company, your growth will proceed through all of these levels.

First, you'll hire another technician. Then an office person and another technician. As you grow, one of your technicians will become the on-location supervisor, or you may have to create one from scratch.

Finally, you'll be able to hire or promote someone to the level of general manager, and you'll probably be running three to four vans.

You probably also will have a thriving rug cleaning operation going at that point and you may end up investing in some dedicated rug cleaning equipment.

You may also do tile cleaning and upholstery cleaning as well.

So You've Got A Million-Dollar Level Three Company... Now What?

It will probably take you around ten to twelve years to get to a level three company, depending upon where you are now.

At that point, you have several options. You of course could sell it. It will probably be worth somewhere in the neighborhood of half a million dollars, depending on the profit it produces for you each year.

In addition to that, you will have the value of any equipment that goes along with the business. This would include things like vans, rug cleaning equipment, etc.

Hopefully by that point, instead of paying rent, you've bought a commercial building and rented it to your business, so your business is paying you rent.

If you sell the business, you can first sign a five-year lease between you and the company, and sell the business with that lease in place. Now you've secured a tenant for your property for another five years.

If you sell the business and the building as a package, then the amount you'll make really depends on how much equity you have in the building. It's not hard to see how you could probably sell the building, the business, and any equipment for close to a million dollars.

Of course, you could just as easily keep the company and manage it... because of the structure, it really won't take much management from you, and the business will probably keep growing on it's own.

This means every year, you'd be able to take more money in profit... and you'd have a business that is worth more money.

When you start to get close to the two million dollar mark, you'll have to make a few investments, and add another couple of mid-level managers.

You usually don't want to stay there, because it's an inefficient place. After you get over the two million-dollar hump, the structure you have at that point will fairly easily take you right up to around the five million-dollar mark.

To grow beyond that, you'll definitely be in the level four area and you'll have departmental managers that are taking care of things. You'll have someone that does human resources etc... In short, you'll have a full-blown company.

This is what that path looks like.

You'll be able to give this to your kids... sell it... or keep it... whatever suits your needs the best.

You'll have money, freedom, and options.

And best of all, it will all be controllable. It won't chase you around the room all of the time.

And while you're building it, you'll have the satisfaction of knowing you're on a path that leads somewhere. You'll know you're building a future for yourself, your family, and quite possibly generations to come.

Why Did I Write This Book?

Because although there are a lot of consultants out there... and it seems nearly everyone has a marketing package to sell these days... no one is showing people this path.

What is being offered to the cleaners are little, disjointed, pieces of this path.

Most of the industry gurus sell packages to 'mom and pop' carpet cleaners, and they do some good for people.

However, it's also true that only about 5% of the people that buy those packages ever really do anything with them.

This idea… this vision… this package, grew out of my exposure, consulting with the largest and most successful carpet cleaning companies on the planet, and it's not like any other package out there because it isn't a solution to a single area like marketing, it's a solution to THE problem facing almost every carpet cleaner out there.

How do you grow your carpet cleaning company into a real business?

This is a path, it's a method, a way of doing business and an approach that will allow you to be truly successful.

Knowing where this path is, and how to walk down it, has tremendous value.

There are three packages that I sell, covering each of the main areas that you'll need to pull this off.

One for sales, one for marketing, and one for management.

I believe that if I can show someone how to make more money from their business, then I deserve some. I mean, that's fair isn't it?

Any one of these packages will easily and quickly pay for itself.

The sales package can double the profit of a company in as little as 28 days. I used to implement this first, because then the increased money from the sales, in effect made the rest of my services free!

The marketing package will allow you to measure and control your marketing and as a result, you'll quit wasting money on ads that don't work. In addition, you'll have the proven techniques that work, so you'll be able to steadily and predictably grow your customer base and keep the customers you've worked so hard to get.

The management system has incredible value in terms of being able to implement and manage these other systems, as well as control quality and control your employees. It also gives you the structure that makes growth possible and manageable. I have had many clients tell me that this is the best place to start, because it provides the structure for everything else.

When you combine these three systems, it really becomes almost an unstoppable force in your business.

You choosing to do this, to go ahead, is a powerful statement of your commitment to build a real business out of what you have now.

Unfortunately, most people can't even manage themselves, much less an organization filled with people that have their own ideas about what they want to spend their days doing!

I wrote this book as a vision... a glimpse of what is possible in this business.

It is impossible to tell you everything in a 200+ page book. The sales system alone contains over 400 pages of single-spaced 8 ½ X 11 sheets, and that's just one section!

What I wanted to do here, was to give you an idea of what's possible, and show you a way to get there.

And now I want to invite you on a journey.

Are you ready to really do this? If you are, I can show you exactly how. It will not always be easy, but it also won't be nearly as hard as you think. Knowing how to get there is half the battle.

Yes, it will cost you some money to do this.

But it truthfully will cost you much more to keep doing what you are probably doing now.

I can't give this to you for free. But it's absolutely cheap compared to what you've already paid to be in this business.

And... since the systems make money very quickly, it's really free after you get even one system up and running!

We won't even consider the cost of lost money and lost opportunity.

We won't consider the blows to your pride and your self-image, when you struggle just to get by or to make ends meet... and they don't!

> "Nothing you can control impacts your life more than a decision"– *Kevin Hogan*

One of two things is going to happen right now:

You can choose to read this message and discredit it... because you'll pretty much have to if you don't take action on it.

It's the only way to justify not spending the money and still make it okay that you didn't!

Or… you'll decide that this is where you want to go.
This will make sense to you.

There are probably a thousand reasons you could come up with to NOT go ahead.

But that's exactly what those are… reasons to NOT MOVE AHEAD! Do you really need those? Are they going to serve you?

I want you to think about something very carefully…

You could realize that there are men that are successful in this industry. In fact, these men are so successful that they could probably buy and sell you many times over.

The most successful people in the world, in this industry… saw this same information… these same concepts that you're seeing right now, and realized the value in it, and willingly paid over $100,000 for it.

It made them many times that within the first year alone!

They then referred me to their friends who did the same thing! For almost ten years I worked strictly by referral.

You DO get to choose… but you also get to live with the consequences of that choice.

It's okay if you don't know how to build a million-dollar business… I mean, why would you? You've probably never done it before have you?

But the real question is, what will you do with the information when it comes?

The time for that decision is right now. Don't put this book down without taking action. If you do, you know as well as I do that you're quite likely to 'get busy' and forget about it... and then six months will go by!

Don't tell yourself that you're going to do it later. It's now... or not at all! Pick up your phone that, if you're a carpet cleaner, is no doubt strapped to your belt and make the call. If money's an issue, we'll work with you.

A Note To Larger Companies

Most programs in the industry are aimed at smaller operators. This can be frustrating for larger companies who might need help with certain areas of their business but who can't find someone that really specializes in larger companies.

All of the systems still apply. They can be easily scaled up for level four companies, in fact, many of the systems won't change at all.

That is the beauty of this system, it is completely scaleable.

In fact, truth be told, many of the systems started out in large companies, and were scaled down for the smaller companies!

A Note To Companies Of All Sizes

Customized Consulting

Even the largest and most successful companies knew they needed help with implementation.

There are many different ways for my organization to work with you. My concept is to find a way for us to partner… to work together on your business. There are many surprisingly affordable ways to do this.

Of course, one of the biggest benefits is that businesses make more money as a result of these systems, my goal is to make them essentially free because of this. In other words, you bring us on, and we'll pay for ourselves! Now THAT'S a deal!

Call my office and talk to someone about it. You'll never know if you don't call!

Toll Free in the USA: **888-245-0001**
Main number: **505-288-3488**

Here's to YOUR success!

Mark Kennedy

levelsofsuccessprogram.com

Be sure and subscribe to the levels of success newsletter for more tips and info on growing your business.

2866451R00126

Printed in Great Britain
by Amazon.co.uk, Ltd.,
Marston Gate.